MW00440901

What's Your Zip Code Story?

What's Your Zip Code Story?

Understanding and Overcoming Class Bias in the Workplace

CJ Gross

ROWMAN & LITTLEFIELD
Lanham • Boulder • New York • London

Published by Rowman & Littlefield
An imprint of The Rowman & Littlefield Publishing Group, Inc.
4501 Forbes Boulevard, Suite 200, Lanham, Maryland 20706
www.rowman.com

86-90 Paul Street, London EC2A 4NE

British Library Cataloguing in Publication Information Available

Library of Congress Cataloging-in-Publication Data
Names: Gross, C. J., 1974- author. | Ross, Howard J., writer of foreword.
Title: What's your zip code story? : understanding and overcoming class
    dynamics at work / CJ Gross ; foreword by Howard J. Ross.
Description: Lanham : Rowman & Littlefield, [2022] | Includes
    bibliographical references and index. | Summary: "Shedding light on
    class division, this book reveals implications and solutions to class bias
    in the workplace by analyzing real experiences, social norms, education,
    wealth, and more"— Provided by publisher.
Identifiers: LCCN 2021047729 (print) | LCCN 2021047730 (ebook) | ISBN
    9781538160589 (cloth) | ISBN 9781538160596 (ebook)
Subjects: LCSH: Discrimination in employment—United States. |
    Classism—United States. | Personnel management—United States. |
    Diversity in the workplace—United States. | Social classes—United
    States.
Classification: LCC HD4903.5.U58 G76 2022 (print) | LCC HD4903.5.U58
    (ebook) | DDC 331.13/30973—dc23/eng/20211230
LC record available at https://lccn.loc.gov/2021047729
LC ebook record available at https://lccn.loc.gov/2021047730

Contents

Foreword

Howard J. Ross

This is a book that has needed to be written for a long time.

Cultures are almost always built around some element of mythology. The stories that we are told, both real and through allegory, are the foundation of what we come to believe about our culture and, correspondingly, our lives. From its earliest days, American culture has rested on the myth of social movement. Long before Horatio Alger wrote about "Ragged Dick" just after the end of the Civil War, the mystique of America has been the notion of equality: the sense that "anybody can make it if they work hard enough." The "up-from-the-bootstraps" story is the core of the American legend. Immigrants have come for years, dreaming about "the streets lined with gold."

America, the land of opportunity.

Yet, as we sit here, still in the early days of the twenty-first century, economic movement in the United States has largely slowed, even among white people. The average person born in the United States will likely move less than one level of the five quintiles of economic class (lower/lower middle/middle/upper middle/ upper) from where he was born, and, according to a recent Brookings Institution study, "Blacks are more likely to stay in the bottom and fall from the middle." The gap between the "haves" and the "have-nots" has widened into a chasm. And our fractured political discourse has the markings of a class struggle.

As someone who has spent the past fifty years working on issues of equity and equality, I have often been shocked by how invisible class has been, in most cases, in so many of these conversations. That's why I am so gratified that CJ Gross does an exceptional job of casting light on this extraordinarily important but largely whispered-about topic. His remarkably open and honest sharing about his personal journey helps us not only understand, but also get a genuine sense of what it is like to experience "class migration." By letting us into his family and his personal journey, and including those of others as well, Gross gives us a narrative that colorizes the data, but also allows us to feel, even if just a bit, what it was like for him and others—and what it is like today for so many in our country.

The powerful gift of this book, however, doesn't stop there. Gross is also able to help us understand the system that we live in. Drawing from sound research and statistical studies, Gross builds a compelling picture of the reality of class in our society. He does an excellent job of looking at the intersectionality of social and seeing how race, gender, and other distinctions of identity influence how the system plays out. By weaving all of this together, he gives us a clear window to see ourselves and how this system has impacted each of us, if we are willing to look.

His narrative helps us understand this system at so many levels: the personal, in our communities, in the workplace, and beyond. The beautiful thing about this book is that it not only helps us understand the underpinnings of the system we live in but also gives us an immensely practical look at how it impacts us in organizations today and what we can do about it.

Read this book. Share this book. And start talking about how class impacts you, your organization, and your community.

Howard J. Ross, a lifelong social justice advocate and founding partner of the nationally recognized diversity consulting firm Cook Ross, Inc., is the author of *Reinventing Diversity: Transforming Organizational Community to Strengthen People, Purpose, and Performance* (2011), *Everyday Bias: Identifying and Navigating Unconscious Bias in Our Everyday Lives,* and *Our Search for Belonging: How Our Need to Connect Is Tearing Us Apart* (2018). His work has been published by the *Harvard Business Review,* the *Washington Post,* the *New York Times,* and *Forbes,* and he has worked with Fortune 500 companies across a variety of industries. He resides in Washington, D.C.

Acknowledgments

We are the authors of our life stories, but much like the anecdotes in this book, the stories of others shape us and can help us write new stories. As with any success in life, writing a book is not a solo performance; it takes a devoted village, a close-knit network, and a trusted support system. For me, that includes my family, friends, mentors, partners, and colleagues, to whom I am deeply grateful.

First, I would like to give my deepest gratitude to my mom, Ella J. Gross. She gave birth to me, nurtured me, gave me the fortitude to dream, and taught me to never settle for second best. Thank you for always believing and instilling the sense that anything is possible. Without your encouragement and relentless inquiry as to when I would complete this book, I would still be writing it instead of sharing it. This book is about uplifting people, something I learned a lot about from you and your lifetime of giving back to others. You have been an unwavering source of love, solace, and support. Thank you, Mom.

To my daughters, Christen and Lauren Gross, know that much of who I strive to be is because of you. Thank you for all your help over the years; I could not have done this without your patience, sacrifices, and hard work; from stocking the vending machines to selling my first books, you always stood by my side and supported me. Your presence in this world has made me a better man; it forced me to consider how I would be a better person, not just for you but for others who look like you. Words cannot express how proud I am of both of you; it's heartening to know that you found your way in life. I am your biggest fan and look forward to supporting, encouraging, and cheering you on as you both have done for me and as you develop into the women you have been divinely created to be.

To my wife, Kerryann Gross, I am blessed to have you in my life and for the close bond, friendship, and love that we share, which grows deeper and stronger every day. Your gentle and not-so-gentle nudges console me and inspire me to reach higher in all that I do. I am ever so grateful for your compassion, generosity, insights, and listening to my book babble. Life with you is like a field of flowers, always budding and blooming with bliss and brightness.

To my editor, Christine Alexy, you made this book a brilliant read and illuminated my words, experiences, and stories. Thank you for writing a winning proposal that helped me land a reputable publisher. I value our collaboration and the diligence, hard work, and long nights you put in to edit, develop, and finish this book by the deadline.

To Charles Tucker, my videographer and graphic designer, thank you for the excellent book cover suggestion and for shooting the TEDx talk that led to this book project. I appreciate all of your efforts and the years of website development and branding design.

To Howard J. Ross, my mentor, friend, and advocate, thank you for bringing me aboard your company, Cook Ross. You kickstarted my career and gave me the opportunity to become an international consultant. I am so very grateful for that, along with your guidance, endorsement, and contributions to this book. I look forward to our continued collaboration and mentorship.

To Dr. Lynn Scott, it's an honor to know you. It's hard to believe four years have passed since we met on the airplane in 2017. Your words of wisdom about leadership, education, and life revealed opportunities, possibilities, and ideas that have since crystallized, possibilities that I would never have considered before our conversations. Thank you greatly for your mentorship; it has broadened my vista and was instrumental in my success as a consultant.

To Chris Morin, my business partner, our meeting was divine from the moment we dined at the Ethiopian restaurant. Although the food was too ornate for my palette, it ignited a deep conversation, leading to a meaningful partnership. I couldn't think of a better person to partner with at Ascension Worldwide. You have taken my consulting firm to the next level, and for that, I am thankful.

To Edward R. Williams, my accountability partner, thank you for helping me meet all my goals. Our accountability partnership kept me on task and committed to everything I said I would do, such as applying to and speaking at the TEDxRushU event in 2019, the prelude to this book. Thanks a million and one for all your encouragement, reassurance, and thoughtful counsel on our coaching calls around business and relationships.

Thank you to all of my friends and colleagues for entertaining my grandiose ideas and backing me as I pursued my dreams of becoming an international speaker, consultant, business owner, author, and everything else I was conspiring to be at that time.

A big thanks to Troy Brown, Lajuan Carter, Renee Cobbs-Colin, Cindy Tawiah, Chris Wilson, Ekaterina Pestekhina, Howard Ross, and Megha Don Bosco for investing the time to interview and sharing your zip code stories. Your contributions impacted me, influencing and cultivating my ideas and foresight and helping to further the authenticity of this book. I will forever be grateful to you for the firsthand insights you each have shared.

To the Speakers Bureau & Event Programming Department at the Society for Human Resource Management (SHRM), thank you for accepting my proposal on Class Bias: The Class Divide in the Workplace and Its Implications. My experience and the outpouring of positive responses at the 2019 SHRM Diversity & Inclusion Conference & Exposition motivated me to write this book. I am proud to be listed in your directory as a recommended speaker.

Thank you to the late Robby Gregg. My conversation with Robert sparked the idea and helped me appreciate that diversity, equity, and inclusion were more about class than race and other identities.

Thank you to my sister and friend, Selina Gross. Knowing each other our entire lives, we have shared many intimate stories of the good, the bad, and the ugly. We don't say it out loud, but please know, Selina, I feel blessed to have had your unconditional love and support over the years. Your tenacity and courage inspired me from the time you chased away the neighborhood bully to your dedication to education, to the hours and hours of "what's possible" conversations, meditation, spirituality, and introduction to the world of coaching.

To my dad, John Francis Gross, who passed away on July 19, 2021, you have inspired me more than you'll ever know. Although your life was absent of simple luxuries, you managed to give me all the things you never had. Thank you for taking me to the motocross track at Budds Creek, fishing and crabbing in Maryland, and to your side jobs when you were an electrician. I'll cherish those moments forever. It meant so much to me to see you cheering me on at my soccer games, attending my speaking engagements, and believing in me enough to invest in my real estate ventures. You were always there to encourage me to your best ability, and you made me feel appreciated. You have been a positive role model; thank you for giving me your all and shaping my life, hopes, and dreams. The memories of our excursions and experiences will live in my heart forever. I continue to live by your principles, heed your advice, and will carry on your legacy. Thank you, Dad. I am proud to be your son. May you rest in peace.

Introduction

What's Your Zip Code Story? illuminates the intersections in our lives, the places that both connect and separate us, the invisible boundaries between the rich and poor, opportunity and choices, truth and perception. The book serves as a looking glass on self and social class. Analogous to the acronym ZIP, or Zone Improvement Plan—this is a guide for class migrant and inclusion improvement, and for workplace diversity. The landmark stories help decode our zip codes and the different cultures, beliefs, experiences, and rules. These are the spaces where we live, fear, collide, and sometimes die. By exploring the similarities in our differences, we can discover our natural biases, see people through a new lens, and enhance our journey.

I was born in the northwest quadrant of Washington, D.C., home to the White House, Georgetown University, the Smithsonian Institution, and other historical landmarks. Although I grew up in Fort Washington, located in Prince George's County, Maryland, one of the wealthiest African American communities in the nation, I was primarily raised by a single mom who worked for the government as a manual laborer. Following in her footsteps, I began working at the ripe age of fourteen as a cashier at a fast-food restaurant—an industry I once believed would be the beginning and end of my story.

At that time, I would have laughed if someone had told me that I would one day become a diversity and inclusion consultant who would embark on a journey across the world and become an author and international speaker.

After years of sweat equity, that's exactly what happened. Today, I not only have a new zip code, but I also have a new story.

For seventeen years, I have trained, coached, and consulted with business and community leaders in the nonprofit, private, and government sectors. Along with growing up in an oyster bed of opportunity, I've had the opportunity to work across various industries.

My work experience includes stints across the automotive, insurance, manufacturing, telecommunications, and engineering fields. Each position taught me something of value. Whether it was operations, production, or customer service, I met different people; learned new processes, procedures, and protocols; and discovered my strengths and weaknesses. I've also led workshops in the medical, legal, education, finance, and human resources fields.

Along my journey, I have traversed continents and countries. Each city, town, and village I visited ignited new possibilities and opportunities. Each added meaning to my life. Whether it was lunch with colleagues in Viña del Mar, Chile, eating porotos granados; singing with strangers from across the world in the oldest Roman amphitheater in Pompeii, Italy; tasting wine with local connoisseurs in Napa Valley; riding bicycles through the city of Barcelona; or having coffee with a colleague in Montgomery County, I was captivated by every new person, sight, smell, taste, custom, language, gesture, and taboo.

Outside of business affairs, my curiosity drove me to meet new people, see new places, and try new things. Chile's Ring of Fire, the most perilous yet powerful place on the planet, could not hold my attention. Most tourists had their eyes glued to the smoldering volcanoes, but every fiber of my being gravitated toward the people. Instead of purchasing volcanic ash or other souvenirs from the gift store, I found myself studying fellow tourists' interactions, tendencies, and communications.

The differences and similarities I discovered within and between each culture can only be described as volcanic. The patterns and parallels were nothing less than astonishing and enlightening. From this zenith, I awoke to a new awareness—a new understanding of people and their perceptions of one another.

Whereas each culture has its own customs, native tongue, and unspoken codes, all share a hierarchy or social class system. I saw it in Canada, working with an oil and gas manufacturer to develop a plan to mitigate bias among distinct Canadian accents. And I saw it while hanging out in Jamaica with my wife, where I realized that those that spoke with English accents were perceived to be educated and of a higher class. Both nuances are embedded in two different cultures, yet they operate in parallel in terms of social class and status, which in this book, I call the "zip code." I'll explain more about my zip code in chapter 2.

HOW THE "ZIP CODE STORY" CAME ABOUT

As a diversity and inclusion consultant, I'm always looking for articles, books, and other relevant information to sharpen my skills and share insights with my colleagues and clients. One day, while surfing the Web, I discovered a thought-provoking *Harvard Business Review* article titled "Why Companies Should Add Class to Their Diversity Discussions." The piece stood out not just because the information was beneficial to my clients, but because I saw myself mirrored in the words of this article.

The article highlighted why companies miss a big part of their diversity and inclusion conversation when they fail to include the topic of social class in their programs. Their research showed that a mere 3 percent of individuals from working-class backgrounds reported that their social class background had not affected their work experiences. That leaves a whopping 97 percent believing that their working-class background affects their work experience. The article was inextricably related to my life and experiences. Ever since I read it, I've had an insatiable hunger to learn more. The article conveyed the many challenges that social class can present, which was all too familiar to me on both conscious and subconscious levels.

A few days after reading the article, I had coffee with a colleague whom I'll call James. He hails from Montgomery County, another wealthy district in Maryland. Our conversation soon turned to the subject of racial bias. Over our second cup, James said that his family was one of the few African Americans in his neighborhood when he was growing up. He went on to tell me that they were denied access to a local country club. As he said it, I could tell that this rejection had burned in the pit of his stomach for some time. Until that day, I never found myself at a complete loss for words with another African American.

Although James and I both grew up in wealthy communities, I could not relate to his country club denial as I had little to no experience engaging in activities outside of my social class. In comparison, I had relatively few racial bias experiences because I was raised in a predominantly African American neighborhood.

As our conversation continued, I realized that race was only half—social class was the other half. Our perceptions on racism and social class differed because we came from different class backgrounds or zip codes. This anomaly validated the article I had just read. I was unable to understand his dilemma because the conversation had expanded beyond race and into social status and social class.

This same scenario plays out in our personal and professional lives. Living in different zip codes does more than separate us by region: it becomes a barrier to establishing communication and building trusting relationships. If we are unable to relate to one another, the conversation usually comes to a screeching halt. When that occurs, we cannot understand the challenges and problems people face, nor can we find commonalities or camaraderie.

In terms of inclusion, diversity, equity and accessibility, if we believe that our primary challenges only pertain to race, ethnicity, sexual orientation, generation, and religion—we're missing a big piece of the puzzle.

A few months after my conversation with James, I facilitated a one-hour discussion about the article at the consulting firm where I worked. That discussion turned into an informal workshop.

I never expected it. Not only did my colleagues welcome the discussion, but they also shared their experiences and perspectives from their different zip codes. The more I listened to their comments and questions, the more I realized the impact of zip code. Social class influences everyone. From the person who answers the phone at the front desk to the CEO, each person had been affected by class and had a unique zip code story.

The deluge of follow-up discussions and e-mails I received proved that the effects of social class had not only elicited an epiphany for me but for what seemed like everyone else. I was on to something.

Once I shared this information with my family and friends, social class and its profound effects were further validated. One family member, whom I'll call Jack, struggled to get promoted at work. Although Jack had earned a college degree, he said he always seemed to be stuck on the bottom rung of the corporate ladder. He was unaware of the rules.

Jack is not the only one who missed the memo and the playbook about unspoken rules. As reflected in the article, many class migrants—men and women—face challenges that hinder their career mobility.

WHAT IS A CLASS MIGRANT?

If you're not familiar with the term "class migrant," let me explain. Although boundaries between classes are often blurry, a class migrant is an individual from the working class who attempts upward mobility to the middle class. The transition is multifaceted. It not only hinges on an individual's shift between educational and occupational status (such as shifting from a semiskilled blue-collar job that requires a high school diploma to a semiprofessional white-collar profession that requires a college degree), but it also hinges on the complexity of switching between cultural and social status spheres. That is, because an individual's identity is shaped by income, occupation, and residential status, he or she has limited to no exposure to the rules and codes of another class. To that end, people from different zip codes or classes (not just races or gender), experience a different social reality, as did James and Jack.

> At the heart of us our social orientation is what drives our lives.
> —Howard Ross, *Our Search for Belonging: How Our Need to Connect Is Tearing Us Apart*

When we are unfamiliar with the social rules in any setting, we are equally unfamiliar with what is or is not appropriate. In a work setting, this not only can make you feel judged and misunderstood, but it could also offend those who are playing by the rules—to the class migrant, invisible rules. Worse, class migrants often feel like they don't belong, making them feel alienated.

Belonging is essential because it is part of our social identity. When we feel like we belong, we are confident, poised, rational, and authentic. On the flip side, when we feel like we do not belong, we often experience insecurity, anxiety, and rejection.

Often, status and success do not remedy feelings of self-doubt. The awareness of differing from others can elicit feelings of inadequacy, which provokes fear of being seen as a fraud—feeling like a phony is known as impostor syndrome, a common phenomenon that occurs when one embarks on a new endeavor or faces a new challenge. Class migrants are particularly susceptible when attempting to join the middle class because they lack exposure to the culture and the codes necessary to succeed in any professional business environment. I will discuss impostor syndrome in depth in a later chapter.

To give you an idea of what changing classes might look like, try to imagine losing your position at the office and having to work in a blue-collar job. One of my colleagues had to step into a different class when she was hired to lead a culture initiative at a manufacturing plant. It would not take an anthropologist to see that the environment was foreign and hostile. Employees not only participated in verbal abuse, but they also got into physical altercations. She was to devise a program to teach employees emotional intelligence, self-regulation, self-awareness, empathy, and kindness—qualities that a professional environment engendered. Although not all blue-collar jobs are this tumultuous, how could she navigate the audience and instill such codes of conduct?

Hard skills are one thing. Soft skills, or business-culture etiquette, for most class migrants are particularly challenging. Soft-skill challenges are so because not only are the rules unspoken, but mind-sets, styles, and mannerisms have been primarily shaped by the rules that govern a working-class culture. We see these dynamics play out when Larry O. Donnell, COO and president of Waste Management, goes undercover at his company. Shortly after assuming the role of garbage collector, Larry is fired from his own organization.

Additional proof of the relevancy of zip codes was evident when I submitted a proposal to speak at the 2019 Society for Human Resource Management (SHRM), a national conference on inclusion. Held in New Orleans, the workshop, "Class Divide in the

Workplace and Its Implications," initially was titled "Class Divide in the Workplace and Its Implications on Diversity and Inclusion." However, although the SHRM committee accepted the topic, it abbreviated the title. I didn't correct them because it was such a great honor to be selected. It was unreal. I was in shock when I learned that I would be speaking alongside some of the top industry experts, especially given that I was not a well-known diversity and inclusion professional at the time.

After months of preparing and rehearsing, I was ready. I was so eager to deliver my speech that I packed my bags weeks beforehand. I felt on top of the world—right up to the day of the conference. As the plane descended into New Orleans, so, too, did my excitement. Nerves got the better of me. While checking into the hotel room, it dawned on me that I had never spoken at a venue of this magnitude. A big lump grew in my throat. In a panic, I began rehearsing. I obsessed over every detail in fear that my lack of experience would be found out—symptoms of impostor syndrome.

Knowing what must be done does away with fear. —Rosa Parks

I tried to remind myself that I was already a national speaker and trainer, but this was different. This was not a scripted speech or workshop through my place of business. This speech was derived from my very own concept. My own material. Me, an African American from Fort Washington, Maryland, with eighteen months of industry experience under my belt.

Up to this point, class was just an interesting conversation. I doubted everything from my abilities to what business I had even being there.

FROM FRAUD TO FAME

Once I arrived, on the first day of a three-day conference, I introduced myself to the participants but withheld the fact that I was a presenter. Although I usually was forthcoming, I was sure that they would see me as a fraud.

The second morning of the conference held a pivotal moment for me. As I stood in line for my cappuccino, I mentioned to a participant that I would be delivering a presentation on social class the next day. Anxious, I did this subconsciously to test the waters. I needed to see the interest in and reaction to my topic. To my surprise, he wanted to hear more.

While I was explaining the premise of my presentation, a woman I'll refer to as Diane overheard our conversation. She immediately approached me with a severe, critical look. Then, out of the blue, she asked if she could hug me.

I paused. I wasn't sure if Diane thought she knew me or if she was executing an uncomfortable introduction exercise. But something inside told me I should consent. We hugged—awkwardly. After we released, I saw tears streaming down Diane's face. She said, "Your topic about class bias is about my life." At one point, she was homeless, addicted to drugs, and a teenage parent. Diane had since earned her doctorate, but she said that class bias remained a significant challenge in her personal and professional life.

She wished me luck and told me my topic was a worthy conversation in the diversity and inclusion space. Our exchange lifted me from the fog of self-doubt and self-criticism.

During lunch that same day, I spoke with Rashida, another conference participant. Two blue-collar parents raised her in a middle-class African American community. Rashida said that although she had attended a private school as a child, she struggled when she entered college and soon after dropped out.

It was not a matter of money or grades, she said. Her parents had a college savings fund set aside, and she had earned above-average grades and SAT scores in high school. Rashida said her decision to drop out was based on a lack of confidence, social fears, and a lack of awareness of how to navigate Ivy League colleges.

Because she was a first-generation college student, she lacked the parental role models and guidance to help her through the college process. Later, I learned that this is common, as "less than 60 percent of students in no-degree families complete their degree."

Rashida's self-doubt led her down a rocky twenty-year road. Absent a degree, she spent the majority of her career in the same position. She decided to pursue a degree after being passed over multiple times for promotion. Over a span of ten years, Rashida earned three degrees, including a doctorate—all while raising three children.

She reflected on how different her life and career would have been had she completed her bachelor's degree earlier. Among other things, the increase in income would have allowed her to save and change her zip code, which would have changed the story of her life and her children's. Although Rashida's lifestyle has improved significantly, she missed twenty years' savings, investment opportunities, and cultural capital.

Her story would have left most people speechless. The exact opposite happened to me. The gravity of this topic seemed to pull both of these stories together. They were all connected to class status and tied tightly to my experiences.

Right then and there, my doubts vanished. I was no longer an impostor. I knew why I was at the conference, and I knew that I belonged there—this was my wheelhouse. Knowing that I was there to share my story and allow others to share their stories, I threw my overly rehearsed presentation to the winds and decided to go off-script.

During the seventy-five minutes, I listened to dozens of class migrant stories of all different races, ethnicities, genders, generations, socioeconomic backgrounds, sexual orientation, and education levels. After eighty minutes, the participants were still passionately sharing their stories. Eventually, the A/V technician grabbed the microphone and shut down the system.

After the presentation, people lined up in the conference room to thank me for giving their stories the space to be heard. A few minutes later, I was again greeted by a line of people in the lobby, thanking me for sharing my story. Within two hours, I had turned from feeling like a fraud to feeling famous.

When I reached the airport to fly home, I spoke with another participant, a young African American man who had completed his bachelor's degree. He was seeking a mentor because he felt stuck in his career. I was flabbergasted—a word I don't use very often.

Then, two women from the conference tapped me on the shoulder to thank me as I boarded my plane. I felt humbled by the abundance of accolades and appreciation I received. Although I knew I was on to something, it was still surreal. I never imagined myself speaking at a conference of this caliber or delivering a topic that so many different people found relatable and relevant.

After returning home to Maryland, I phoned my older sister, Selina, to tell her about my experience in New Orleans. During our discussion, Selina decided to share her class migrant story. Although I was aware of my sister's acceptance at Howard University, we never discussed why she chose not to attend. Sadly, I was not surprised to learn that Selina did not pursue her dream college because she saw it as an unrealistic feat and felt intimidated by the arduous application process. Like Rashida, my sister was a first-generation student and, therefore, lacked the push and guidance from our parents. Because of this, Selina decided to attend a community college. Although Selina later earned a master's degree from the University of Illinois, to this day she struggles with upward career mobility—again, not surprising.

Speaking with my sister made me recall my father's story. After serving in the army during the Vietnam War, his commanders nominated him to attend West Point. Back in the day, he told me that he forwent the opportunity because his family did not encourage it—they lacked the understanding of its value. To this day, I wonder what kind of opportunities Selina and I would have had if my dad had pursued and earned a degree from West Point.

Sometimes the webs we weave are merely extensions of the webs already spun. I have come to realize that I, too, missed opportunities. I was offered an entrepreneur scholarship that would have led to a bachelor's degree from the University of Maryland, but at the time, I believed such ambition was out of reach. Later I will share more about my own zip code story.

WHO SHOULD READ THIS BOOK?

This book centers on real stories designed to help you reflect on your zip code story. I will draw on examples from historical figures, the stories of other class migrants, and my own to provide insights about our zip codes and how all of our stories collectively affect both our personal and professional life.

Individuals seeking career growth; professionals who are developing initiatives in the inclusion, diversity, accessibility, and equity space; people managers; and all class migrants should find this book beneficial. Accompanying the class migrant stories, I will present the power of belonging, strategies for class migrant career mobility, techniques that managers can implement to help class migrants succeed, and why mentorship matters.

I hope this book inspires you, informs you, and helps you implement its ideas and concepts for self-growth and enlightenment. Enjoy the read!

1

Why Does Social Class Matter . . . So Much?

Move before you are ready. Most people wait too long to go into action, generally out of fear. They want more money or better circumstances. You must go the opposite direction and move before you think you are ready. It is as if you are making it a little more difficult for yourself, deliberately creating obstacles in your path. But it is the law of power that your energy will always rise to the appropriate level. When you feel that you must work harder to get to your goal because you are not quite prepared, you are more alert and inventive. This venture has to succeed and so it will.[1]
—50 Cent and Robert Greene, *The 50th Law*

Social class drives human behavior. Whether or not we believe it, class structures our society.

Our names often reveal our social class and the heritage that our predecessors pass on. The Kennedys, Rothschilds, and Rockefellers are modern-day aristocrats—considered upper upper class, their family names carry a pedigree of nobility, power, and influence.

Our ears perk up, and we tend to pay homage to those who hold such prestige. Years ago, a colleague of mine mentioned his uncle's entrepreneurial skills. Before he dropped his name, I knew that he was a famous billionaire. No further details about his business expertise were necessary. I clung to his every word. Reginald F. Lewis's name spoke for itself. He had earned a football scholarship to Virginia State University, graduated from Harvard Law with a juris doctorate, and established Wall Street's first African American law firm. Then he became the first African American to build a billion-dollar company. Lewis was also counsel for the New York-based Commission for Racial Justice.[2]

Lewis was a visionary. All revered him, and his business and finance acumen were highly commendable. Although he passed away at the early age of fifty, his family legacy remains a potent inspiration. Lewis's parents and grandparents taught him how to save money; perhaps more telling of his success, they encouraged him to "be the best that you can be."[3] The inspiration and certainty of accomplishment, if you imagine, believe in yourself, work hard, and seek ways to make a difference, championed both Reginald and his half brother, Jean S. Fugett Jr., a former all-star for the Dallas Cowboys and Washington Redskins. Fugett later became a lawyer and joined forces with his brother at the TLC Beatrice International Holdings Inc., a major international food processing company.[4] The Olympic-size torch of inspiration, education, and success was passed to Fugett's children and Lewis's two daughters, Christina and Leslie.

People are born into a social class. We make decisions on education, occupation, relationships, reproduction, neighborhoods, clothing, diet, and vacation destinations based on class. Although individuals are not "assigned" to a lifelong occupation or social position, as is the case with a caste system, class profoundly affects how people live, the type of work they will likely do, and their income.

An open class system pivots on two tethered forces: social factors and individual achievement. If not counterbalanced, the former limits the latter.

Meritocracy tips the scale. The American Dream—the "ideal" that personal effort alone determines success and social class—is a belief that social factors play no role in achievement. The widely held notion that individual effort *alone* determines one's social status arises from one's social class experience, level of awareness of his or her inherited cultural capital, and support network that assists in achieving personal and professional goals. School grading systems and employee performance appraisal methods teach us that our own efforts—our individual merits are what get us there.

Just as culture is not visible to its holder, "privilege is not visible to its holder; it is merely there, a part of the world, a way of life, simply the way things are."[5] Class is no different. We don't see ourselves as part of the upper class or lower class—we just are. But make no mistake: all of us can detect when others are from a different culture and social class than our own.

Class is measured in terms of socioeconomic status, including one's level of education, occupation, and income. Each is tangible and acts as a scaffold or stepping-stone to the next tier. It's challenging to think about the intangibles—the scaffolds that support each step of each stepping-stone.

Lewis's daughters appreciate the scaffolding that supports their success. But as men, we often don't see the scaffolding that supports our success. We put all of our efforts into our profession to secure our position and earn promotions—the upward mobility of ourselves and our families.

> If I have seen further, it is by standing on the shoulders of giants.[6]
> —Isaac Newton

Effort is influenced by our ability, interest, experience, opportunity, self-belief, and resource or situational constraints. By default, effort will decrease if one of these forces is deficient or absent. Because of our individualistic American culture and the systems that support it, we tend to see our efforts, successes, and corresponding privileges as fruits of our own merit.

Consider time and resources and their possible constraints on opportunity from John's perspective.

> I was able to earn a bachelor's of business administration and start my life with little student debt. My father paid nearly half of my tuition, and my mother had the time and resources to make sure I was well-rounded. As a father and married man, I have the privilege to leave for work early because my wife ensures the children get to school on time. I arrive at my desk with focus, energy, and discretionary time to network, innovate and even polish my presentations if I want. I am free of the household burdens of cleaning, laundry, shopping, errands and bill paying. My dry cleaning is picked up, and I am not constrained by domestic duties such as doctor appointments for the children or helping with homework, filling out school records, or working on crafts for school projects. I am fortunate that my wife takes care of all and the particulars involved, as well as my children's social affairs and playdates. She teaches them morals and life lessons and takes care of their emotional needs. She manages their hygiene, routines, rules, and

expectations and runs the household schedule. She also encourages them to do things that are in their best interests, like pushing them to earn top grades, involving them in volunteer opportunities, and teaching them responsibility, teamwork and accountability by ensuring they make it to every sporting practice and game. My wife has essentially taken on the duties that my mother once filled. Her parenting, nurturing, discipline, coaching, and mentoring prepares our children to thrive, which for all intents and purposes gives them a competitive advantage in college and in the business world.

While all this is happening on her watch—I'm at work, which gives me the time and competitive edge to talk shop—develop key relationships, gain business insights from colleagues and people of influence after work. In the early years of my career, my wife stayed home while I traveled for business and leadership seminars. I also had the good fortune of taking night courses where I earned an MBA. I basically operated independently. My wife always managed to leave work early when the children were ill. When the children were sick for more than a day, she used her personal days or asked the children's grandmother to watch the children. Because she has a lower earning potential than me, she assumes all of these roles. Though I tried, I never had to be home to cook dinner, attend school conferences or chorus concerts. Most evenings, I could relax and watch sports because she was there to drive the children to the doctor, extracurricular activities, or pick up that red T-shirt that the school requested last minute.

To say that I am where I am today because of my own doing, my own effort, my own merits—*alone*—is to say that my grandparents, parents, wife, professors, mentors, colleagues, friends, and managers played no part in my success. When in fact, each served me—invested in me and supplied their time, energy, support, connections, and knowledge—giving me the opportunity to perform well, be productive and climb the corporate ladder.[7]

Those people are John's scaffolding—the intangibles that seed social class. Somewhere deep inside, we know this to be true. The first words out of our mouths after we graduate from college, get a promotion, write a book, or survive cancer is, "I could not have done this without you."

> None of us got where we are solely by pulling ourselves up by our bootstraps. We got here because somebody—a parent, a teacher, an Ivy League crony or a few nuns—bent down and helped us pick up our boots.[8] —Justice Thurgood Marshall

Nonetheless, heritage, economic opportunities, cultural capital, and social class have a reciprocal influence on one another, guiding our actions.

As class influences opportunities, so it influences our choices and decisions. For example, a lower- and working-class person may not consider engaging in a specific sport, such as squash. For one, a sport such as this is not a typical cultural pastime. Even if a class migrant desires to play squash (a sport that provides excellent intercultural social opportunities), chances are he or she would not have the means to get into a private club or squash court. In other words, squash is not in that person's line of vision.

When something seems exclusive, the perception is that it must be better. This perception flows from class-bias thinking. The *Harvard Business Review* article "Why Companies Should Add Class to Their Diversity Discussions" holds that class is expressed through cultural differences, not just how much money is in your bank account. For example, what are elite sports? Polo, tennis, windsurfing, squash. What are working-class sports?[9] Although it may be hard to accept that class drives us, it does. Class is the invisible structure that divides all and drives some. In extreme cases, class decides who eats and who does not, who lives and who does not.

Class society has prevailed from classical antiquity to twenty-first-century civilization. Primarily instituted to maintain wealth and keep order, each class by default can be thought of as an in-group—cheering those who belong, booing those who do not. Whether you are from the working class, lower class, middle class, or upper middle class, we all strive to belong to a higher class primarily because with it comes privilege. Sometimes people risk it all in the name of class status.

Case in point: in early 2019, wealthy parents, actresses, administrators, and elite athletic coaches were convicted for their participation in a massive college admissions and exam scandal. William Rick Singer, CEO of a college admissions prep company, not only orchestrated the scam, accepting $25 million to bribe university officials, "his goal," as he said, "was to help the wealthiest families in the U.S. get their kids into school."[10]

For many, the idea of the wealthy using their status, position, or money to cut corners comes as no surprise. The unscrupulous lengths to which these parents sank in efforts to get their children into Ivy League schools paint a bigger picture. The risk alone reflects that although these parents had some assets, they were not all that wealthy—otherwise, their children could have had tutelage or could rest on their parents' laurels. The choice to take part in criminal acts, possibly risk a jail sentence and one's position in life, shows us the power of class status and its influence on our decisions. In other words, these parents engaged in unethical and illegal behaviors in an attempt to buy social privilege for their children.

Again, we all strive for things we perceive as valuable. Acceptance into Yale and Stanford are highly sought for good reasons—all rooted in class. Children who graduate from an Ivy League university are associated with a respected brand of academia, which bolsters their esteem, character, and social networks and elevates their respect, social status, and privilege.

Unfortunately, keeping up with the Joneses has never been as arduous as it is today. Even those who are well off find that the education bar has been raised to new heights. Education is a significant barrier to higher class status, but it is only one of many.

HOW IS SOCIAL CLASS MEASURED?

The government measures class based on socioeconomic status. For the purposes of this book, we will measure class by criteria such as education, occupation, and income, along with wealth, power/influence, culture, heritage, and prestige. This list is more reflective of how society measures and perceives social class.

Individuals and companies put a great deal of value on education and where it is received. Several aspects of education connote class. For example, if one attends an Ivy League university, others assume that he possesses the financial means to pay for this type of education and has the comparable book smarts.

Yearly income is another indicator of class. The more money you earn, the more money you can save and invest. In addition, the more money you make, the more likely that you'll have disposable income for continuing education and status symbols such as luxury cars, name-brand goods, country club memberships, and trips to exotic islands.

One's occupation (job or profession) can signify educational status and earning potential. Job and profession are two different things. A job is akin to a trade; manual labor or the service industry, which is paid by the hour, such as retail or a job as a plumber, waitress, janitor, and mechanic. A profession is associated with a career or salaried position such as a manager, doctor, accountant, lawyer, stockbroker, or architect. For example, it would be unlikely to see a gastrointestinal surgeon working for an hourly wage at a McDonald's.

Wealth is your accumulated net worth minus debt. Wealth encompasses all material assets, including income, real estate, stocks, trusts, and bonds. If an outstanding debt exists on material items; once the debt is subtracted from the value, that is the amount of wealth that particular item holds for the owner.

Power is an interesting measure of social class because each of us has some degree of it. Power is influence or the ability to make something happen. Wealth is a source of power, but power also comes in the form of position, including legitimate, coercive, or reward power; expert and informational power (possession of knowledge and skills); connection power (association with someone of influence); referent power (respect endorsed by others when one is well liked);[11] and personal power (radiated positive energy).

> The most common way people give up their power is by thinking they don't have any.[12] —Alice Walker

When the president of the United States wants something to happen, he holds positional or legitimate power to accomplish the mission at hand. Some presidents use coercive power such as imposing sanctions or tariffs on other countries to achieve results. Managers also hold positional power; they can grant or deny promotions, give or take away bonuses. Team leaders, teachers, and police also have positional power.

Other sources of power include attractive appearance or the position in your company, family, or community. These are all different flavors of power. If you can go to work tomorrow and ask your manager for a week off and your coworkers cannot, referent power is at work. A manager who compensates one employee over another might be enacting reward power, if the employee performed exceedingly well; or coercive power based on disapproval of behavior, such as taking away privileges. Referent power is in play when employees respect their manager and volunteer to take on extra work. Referent and reward power can work both ways, such as when a manager likes an employee or perceives that she is attractive and offers mentorship, perks, or leniency.

A combination of other aspects of class can increase one's power and influence dramatically. Imagine Joe. He is a director, good looking, well dressed, has a high level of education, and is persuasive in articulating his thoughts and ideas. We typically don't break it down this way, but Joe possesses many forms of power—including personal power. This gives Joe a certain level of social status or clout within the company. Like society, organizations have their own social class hierarchy.

Not everyone can be good looking, but each of us holds personal power. Personal power can garner all other forms of power. As unique individuals with unique experiences and perceptions, we are experts in unique information and domains. We also experience unique adversities. Some encounter occasional hardships, whereas others are more intimate with hardships. In the face of adversity, each of us develops a proportional degree of resilience and endurance to adapt and overcome obstacles.

Class migrants receive more than their share of training on adversity and resilience.[13] They come to the table with authentic leadership and soft skills that cannot be easily taught: perseverance, insights, creativity, and resourcefulness—it's embedded in their very being. Outside perspectives are fresh perspectives. Because of their class experiences, class migrants are self-reliant and confident solution seekers. They are similar to hiring a third-party consultant agency to detect, isolate, and resolve a problem, but class migrants are more actively aware of the overarching efficiencies and inefficiencies than others within an organization, who often are too close to see a problem or grasp it. Authenticity, leadership, confidence, grit, and ingenuity are qualities of personal power.

Culture is fascinating; although we all are tied to a primary one, we rarely think of it as a factor of class. For this book, class includes the acceptable social norms in one's environment. If you grew up in a household where your parents argued and raised their voices at one another regularly, you may find yourself arguing and raising your voice to others around you. It's your norm. You may not even be aware that raising your voice is part of your culture because it is acceptable and normal to you—until someone from a different culture points it out.

Culture is a combination of material and nonmaterial things. It is in our practices, customs, traditions, and activities including art, religion, poetry, music, dance, sports, foods, exercise, values, beliefs, and taboos. Culture lies in our style, preferences, habits, and pastimes: storytelling, reading books, word choice, dialect, profanity; wearing tight jeans, baggy pants, hoodies, or khakis, suit and tie, or loafers. Culture is in our leisure activities: visiting the symphony, watching TV or movies, skiing, hiking, fishing, traveling, and playing chess or Words with Friends.

These cultural nuances differ among different levels of social class and notably serve as social class cues as people engage. Culture can be subtle. It is detected in our eye contact, posture, and gait, in preferences for water versus soda, or fast food versus dining in. That is, our "behaviors and cultural practices are infused with social class and, as a result . . . communicate social class position to observers."

> Understand: people judge you by appearances, the image you project through your actions, words, and style. If you do not take control of this process, then people will see and define you the way they want to, often to your detriment. You might think that being consistent with this image will make others respect and trust you, but in fact it is the opposite—over time you seem predictable and weak. Consistency is an illusion anyway—each passing day brings changes within you. You must not be afraid to express these evolutions. The powerful learn early in life that they have the freedom to mold their image, fitting the needs and moods of the moment. In this way, they keep others off balance and maintain an air of mystery. You must follow this path and find great pleasure in reinventing yourself, as if you were the author writing your own drama.[14]

In our society, conversations about culture can quickly lead to the topic of race. For this book, I only use the term race when it applies in context to avoid stereotypes or any connotation that race equals culture, because it does not.

Many times, our work culture is different from our personal culture. Although we wear different hats for different occasions, there are common threads. For example, my dad was an electrician, and his coworkers used profanity and drank beer after work. On many occasions, my dad exhibited these same behaviors at home, which did not blend with our home culture. Our culture reflects our perceptions about others and ourselves in the world.

Prestige is the respect or admiration ascribed to someone. It refers to esteem or the approval for exemplary acts, deeds, or qualities. Prestige is cultural capital. It's frequently associated with the social status of the upper class, and it gives people a sense of worth and respect, which, in turn, is transformed into social and economic advantage.

Different cultures consider different things prestigious. An engineering degree from MIT is valued more in an international construction management firm than a diploma from a trade school or community college. In contrast, wearing the latest "Jordans" in specific urban neighborhoods in the United States is viewed as prestigious. Although both exemplify prestige, each is based on the values held within that class culture.

Each class has its own social hierarchy, and classes sometimes borrow cultural materials to symbolize social standing. Class sometimes means taking expensive extracurricular hip-hop dance classes in suburban areas or driving a luxury Lincoln in urban neighborhoods. Each signifies status and prestige in their respective regions, and each conveys a particular class outside their regions. Think about that for a moment.

On the one hand, hip-hop connotes lower and working class, the culture from which it originated. However, when commodified and performed in a hip-hop dance showcase, it connotes upper middle class. The same can be said for driving an expensive car. Driving a newer BMW in a wealthy region can convey that a person is from the upper middle or upper class—or sometimes living beyond their means. But driving a BMW in an impoverished area can connote two different things depending on who observes it and the shape the car is in. Whether new, used, or dented, if the BMW has dark tinted windows, a person from the lower or working class may perceive that the driver is of an upper middle or upper class—but only within that community's social hierarchy. Yet, a driver in that exact vehicle in a wealthy community may be perceived as lower class. Lived experiences have a more significant impact on class division than the economic constraints of social class.

MONEY CAN'T BUY CLASS

Some people believe that class, like a material item, can be bought. Nothing could be further from the truth. In reality, possession of money and material things only makes up a small portion of social class—again, class cannot be bought.

Cindy Tawiah knows this better than anyone. Native to the upper-class part of Ghana, Africa, Cindy was able to attend a boarding school in London, England. Growing up in two different countries gives her unique insights into class, culture, and people's perceptions about money and why it cannot buy class or genuine respect.

> When you go to England, [*sic*] rather, when I grew up in London in particular, it was very well known that people who came from the East End were not educated. They were blue collar, and those who came from the West End, South, and the North, they were more the uppity. And in England, you can have a lot of money and not have respect. They view them as the nouveau riche. Nouveau riche [*sic*] means new money. Experiencing how people viewed true social class, not just money, had an indelible impact on my upbringing that also shapes the way I see the world today. (Cindy Tawiah, interview by author, "How growing up in two different countries gives her unique insights into class, culture, and people's perceptions about money and why it cannot buy class or genuine respect," n.d.)

Cindy also talks about her family culture from Ghana, bringing awareness of the sacrifices and hardships of a multicultural zip code. She said:

> many Ghanaians who live and work in London must send money back home to support brothers, sisters, family members, and extended family members in Ghana. My father told his brothers and sisters not to contact me [*sic*] or his other children for anything, to leave us alone, not basically become burdens on us. This is the challenge of having a multicultural zip code story. You are never just from one culture; there are many things that make up who you are and how you see the world.

Class is also subjective. It's relative to whom an individual compares himself in the social hierarchy—even those with income levels of $250,000 who fall in the upper class sometimes see themselves as upper middle class. That is, people tend to compare themselves to the classes directly above and below theirs. It makes sense then that those earning $250,000 might see themselves as upper middle class compared to those who earn $500,000 or more. Likewise, those who earn $250,000 may see themselves as upper class compared to those who earn $100,000 or less.

The point is, we are socialized and conditioned by the class culture in which we reside. Our income, occupation, education, experiences, preferences, clothing choices, beliefs, behaviors, and activities are all telltale signs of class. Our class is in our posture, gait, eye contact, accent, inner circles, zip code, and residential status (renter or owner). These nuances not only shape our class, but they also reveal our class to the people around us. It is human nature to draw inferences about others based on these characteristics—this is why class and status cannot be bought. Comparisons and inferences are related to what researchers call "social class signals—behaviors that provide information about a person's income, educational attainment, or occupation status.[15] They also suggest that people are shaped by class in their everyday interactions, and the social class signals they perceive from other classes shape their psychological experience.

Class and culture can be absorbed, developed, and learned—after all, we were born and raised in a certain social class. We know class can be absorbed because we've seen immigrants assimilate or become acculturated to the United States. We know this because we've seen the poor become rich and adapt to their new class—John Paul DeJoria (cofounder, Paul Mitchell), Oprah Winfrey, and Howard Schultz (CEO, Starbucks). It is unnecessary to learn or do everything the upper class does. Still, it is necessary to understand the nature and nuances of different classes, especially if you desire upward social and career mobility.

We don't elect our class; others assign a class to us. Simply being from a particular region or speaking a different dialect can elicit stereotypes. For example, Renee Collins Cobb, a white woman of Appalachian heritage from the Bluegrass State, experienced microaggressions and class bias in the way people treated her Southern accent. She said when she moved from Kentucky to Ohio, people at work tended to believe "we all married our cousins, we are related to everyone else in Kentucky, and we were hillbilly—a stereotype that has come to equate with unintelligent, backwards, early pregnancy, barefoot, and no teeth." Stereotypes constrain people. For Renee, being a Kentuckian made upward mobility a colossal challenge. Many in her situation don't escape poverty, but she accepted the challenge head-on. Today, Renee holds a master's degree in human resources development, is a VP of professional development, and is a consultant partner at Cook Ross.

Understanding different social classes and norms makes it easier to engage and operate in different social classes, supporting personal and professional goal attainment. Beyond income and educational status, we can better assimilate to the social class we aspire to join by engaging in the cultural activities of that class.

As with any relationship or social group, people are accepted when they are liked—and liked when they share common interests. Not everyone has to like you, but likability can open doors that are otherwise closed. Successful leaders and managers have two things in common: likability and leverage. They develop trusting relationships with their employees, clients, and colleagues. Referent power is gained when one gets to know someone as a person, remembers the names of and asks about her family, and learns about her likes and dislikes. Successful leaders not only arrive early for work and perform well, but they also make it their job to talk about the activities, hobbies, and interests of their peers, customers, and clients.

But to talk about it and benefit from it, you must get involved and gain experience. This could mean taking up or teaching yourself golf, crossbow, biking, running, or working out at a popular gym. Low-cost activities include watching TED Talks every week or taking thirty minutes each night to read business classics such as *How to Win Friends and Influence People* by Dale Carnegie, *Living the Seven Habits: The Courage to Change* by Stephen R. Covey, *Start with Why* by Simon Sinek, or *Who Moved My Cheese?* by Spencer Johnson. These are character builders, conversation sparkers or conversation keepers (as I like to call them). Humor is another effective way to facilitate camaraderie because it allows you to share your personality and resilience to criticism, and to get sincere opinions.

These activities improve communication and your ability to connect and adapt to a higher class. And they present the opportunity to build the relationships and referent power needed for further personal and professional growth. Participating in activities that your coworkers like allows you to strike up a conversation with them, relate to them, and eventually enter their circle and gain access to business insights. Once you have established a rapport, seek out mentorship opportunities and volunteer for team projects, both internal and external to your department. Make opportunities by finding a need and taking the initiative to fill it. Get involved (find a problem and offer a solution). Ask or get invited to key meetings. Get noticed. And repeat with maniacal consistency. When you interact outside your "social class" at work, you can learn new skills and gain exposure to different business operations and opportunities. This draws your mind and scope of work out of the weeds and directs your attention to long-term goals, strategic thinking, and a broader horizon.

When it comes to social class, whether at home or work—your activities speak volumes.

The most effective way to acculturate from a lower to higher social class is to change your zip code. Although challenging, keep in mind that you have faced and overcome much more complex challenges in life. With a new place and an open mind, changing your zip code can improve your perspective and increase your possibilities and opportunities. It can provide access to upper-class resources and activities, community volunteer engagement, and firsthand class-cultural exchanges and experiences—the same as it can in the workplace—all culture, character, and career building blocks.

I know women who listen to sports radio on the way to work just so they have material for banter in the good ol' boys club. It's an informal social and support network. where alliances are formed with like-minded individuals and information and knowledge are shared about high-visibility enterprise projects, organizational politics, business strategies, and unpublicized opportunities. These networks are socially connected to those in higher positions and are often critical to climbing the ladder.

> The richest people in the world look for and build networks, everyone else looks for work.[16] —Robert Kiyosaki

In a business environment, even the everyday humdrum experiences can create a shared reality. Conversation starters come with ease when we have read the same books or played the same sports. It's even easier when we live in the same community. Our realities align when we can relate to those I-95 traffic jams by the airport, that bottleneck near the university, long lines at the Starbucks, or the restoration progress of that historical farmhouse on the way to the running trail. Icebreakers such as these are helpful around the water cooler; conversation keepers will pull you closer to the social networks that can boost your career. Take a look around. No matter what class you are from, people like like-minded people.

What makes networking work is that it sets up win-win situations in which all parties involved get to take something home. Networking is a sharing process. Until you understand that, you won't have much of a network.[17] —Earl G. Graves

Self-perception matters. Years ago, I worked with a mentoring program operated by two seasoned entrepreneurs who believed that true success derives from perception. One of the partners said something that stuck with me: "If you can't see it, you can't be it."[18] This adage is true. Reginald Lewis had this same visionary mentality. His eldest daughter, Leslie, an actress, writer, producer, and businesswoman, said, "He taught me and my sister how to visualize something and then allow it to happen."[19] Lewis's daughters saw it and allowed it to happen. Christina is a Harvard graduate and founder of a leading not-for-profit organization, All Star Code—lauded by the Obama administration as a champion of change for STEM access.

People tend to mimic successes they see. Some people go out of their way to establish class status among their peers and those they don't know. Driving a $100,000 electric car, strutting in designer red-bottom shoes, or living in an upscale community are all acts rooted in class. I've known people who purchased imitation Rolexes or Gucci handbags in attempts to appear of a higher class. But these objects are merely aesthetic. Materials do not change the social rules that you have lived by or your social capital and practices. When it comes to class status, mimicking the material culture of those in a higher class can be counterproductive without emulating their demeanor or nonmaterial culture. In the introduction, we saw the impact of unspoken rules and how they can affect the brightest of us, even those who have earned Ivy League college degrees such as Jack, Diane, and Rashida. They all struggled with upward career mobility. To this day, despite earning a master's degree from the University of Illinois, my sister, Selina, lags in her career.

Although I will not draw conclusions about the reasons for their challenges, there is little doubt that social class played a significant role in their outcomes. I am not speaking about biases against *individuals themselves*. I am speaking about the nonmaterial culture, the lack of understanding and playing by the social-class rules, and the skills essential to rise and gain respect within a professional business culture such as negotiation, referent power, and influential relationships. That is, to succeed in raising your class status, you must not only have educational credentials and obtain a position within a company, but you must immerse yourself in the business community and harness the protocols of that class culture. As we learn the modes and codes of class, the doors to success open a little wider. We learn by doing. And we do by believing.

> Self-confidence doesn't spring from external accomplishments. Instead, it arises from internal certainties.[20] —Christina Lewis

When we think of heritage, we think of the properties we inherit or the recipes and heirlooms passed down through the generations. However, we usually overlook the fact that we inherit our culture, knowledge, philosophies, and possibilities. That is, our heritage not only consists of monetary assets or possessions inherited from our ancestors; it consists of the invisible and involuntary attributes—the ascribed status that both creates and shapes our character and culture. This includes everything from our beliefs to our ideologies, values, mannerisms, traditions, social class, and perceived lot in life. All of these sculpt our vistas.

Reginald Lewis and his daughters are examples of how our perceptions shape our vistas, visions, and vernacular.

Boiled down, social class is a way of being, thinking, doing, and creating. Social class is not for sale, but the nuances of different cultures can be observed, learned, and subsequently adopted.

CLASS MIGRANTS

Social class affects everyone, but it has a more significant impact on class migrants. The previously mentioned article published by the *Harvard Business Review* identifies class migrants as individuals who grow up in one social class but find themselves at some point in life (due to education, career choices, or other situations) in a different class. For example, I grew up in a lower-class household. My dad was an electrician; my mom, a weapons specialist. Both worked for the federal government. Neither of my parents held a college degree, unlike most of my friends' parents in my neighborhood. Some of their parents had advanced degrees.

Not only did our monetary and material possessions differ from our neighbors; so did our conversations around the dinner table. For instance, my parents would ask what I would do to support myself after high school. In contrast, my friends' parents would ask which college they wanted to attend to prepare for their careers. These questions alone serve as cues and set the tone for what is expected and accepted in our families.

My socialization process began much earlier. While I faced pressure to work and supplement income at an early age, my friends faced pressure to study, earn top grades, and hone skills in an elite sport. Given their parental guidance, my friends learned about finances, goal setting, negotiation, persuasion, and the importance of building influential relationships.

The expectations that our parents set and the life stories that they share as we develop shape the lens of our beliefs, visualizations, and possibilities—sometimes the course of our lives.

Whatever our parents' lineage, they teach us what they know to prepare us to survive, compete, and thrive in our social class. My parents lacked exposure to the middle class. However, my friends' parents had assimilated to the dominant culture of the corporate world. They had the wherewithal to prepare and groom their children for the corporate world from the onset. In doing so, they taught, stressed, and reinforced the importance of attire, articulation, appearance, etiquette, and behaviors that are acceptable, appropriate, and representative of the professional community and business culture.

These drastically different schools of thought are part of the reason class migrants experience culture shock and feel disoriented when pursuing an Ivy League college education. It's also why they struggle to establish themselves in the middle and upper class and climb the rungs of the corporate ladder.

Robert Kiyosaki's best-seller, *Rich Dad, Poor Dad*, chronicles his upbringing and conversations with his biological dad and his best friend's dad.[21] He called his biological father "Poor Dad" because of how he thought and approached work and business. He called his friend's father "Rich Dad" because of how he thought and approached work and business. Robert's biological dad was formally educated but did not know how to build wealth. In contrast, Robert's friend's father had no formal education but knew how to grow a business and wealth. The two dads were great fathers, but Robert realized that talking to one dad would lead to working for someone else, which would provide limited income potential, but talking to the other dad would lead him to wealth and a real estate empire. Absent the input of both dads, Robert most likely would not be an author and millionaire today. His career would have been constrained, parallel to his birth father's experience.

Early in life, I made educational and career decisions based on my parents' background, experiences, and conversations. They were my compass; their social class, my vista.

I learned that to be successful at class migration, I must learn a new set of rules that are polar opposites from the rules that I was taught as a child. The *Harvard Business Review* article mentioned earlier in this book shared an eye-opening statistic: "Research shows 61% of college enrollees in 2011–2012 were from households that didn't have a bachelor's degree holding parent. That is over half of today's rising workforce. By failing to acknowledge the importance of class background in workplace culture, organizations are risking their future—a future that's already arrived."[22]

When class migrants finally complete their degree, they face a steep learning curve in adapting to life after college. Not only do *all* new graduates graduate with more hard skills than soft skills[23] (the skills valued in today's global economy), but class migrants do not have a clear road map to make the best use of their academic education.

Because of this, when they enter the workforce, they often flounder. On top of that, the rules instilled during a class migrant's developmental stage do not apply to their new work culture. Many class migrants encounter a culture clash and do not make it past the gatekeepers, especially because employers tend to seek employees who are like-minded and "fit the culture." If they are offered a position, they frequently find themselves in a static position, unable to move the needle on their career.

The upside is that many class migrants are resilient, resourceful, and have abundant real-world experience. The downside is that businesses fail to recognize and leverage those transferrable skills and abilities. Unfortunately, even with a degree, without knowledge of the middle- to upper-class rules, class migrants lag in their careers, income, class, and often, life itself.

2

My Zip Code Story

Don't give others the chance to pin you down; keep moving and changing your appearances to fit the environment. If you encounter walls or boundaries, slip around them. Do not let anything disrupt your flow.[1] —50 Cent and Robert Greene

We'll begin this chapter with a short introduction. Then I'll share my parents' story because it's essential to understand how they influenced my dreams, beliefs, and decisions in my formative years.

I was raised in 20744, the zip code assigned to Fort Washington, Maryland. Adjacent to Washington, D.C., today Fort Washington is an upper-middle-class, African American neighborhood. It borders the National Harbor, an international tourist attraction, minutes from landmarks such as the Smithsonian Institution and the U.S. Capitol.

In the 1700s, Fort Washington protected Washington, D.C. It was here that George Washington lost a battle to Great Britain. Before the migration of African Americans from Washington, D.C., to Fort Washington, the 20744 zip code was predominantly white.

Migrants flocked to the historic Fort Washington because of its well-paid federal jobs. My parents moved my sister, Selina, and me here in the 1970s. Although settling into a new area is often easier for children, it took some time to adapt to our new environment and what was to become of our family. At that time, Fort Washington was still segregating its school system. Being African American meant that Selina and I were bussed to an elementary school in a neighboring city.

My most illuminating memories trace back to the 1980s, a confusing time in which my parents separated. Far from the then-model Huxtable family, depicted in the iconic sitcom *The Cosby Show*, Selina and I were brought up in a single-parent household. Although my father was a stone's throw away, the one-income household began to shape my awareness of money. I was old enough to understand that our material possessions and activities differed from our neighbors. Plus, when dad came to visit, he never missed an opportunity to remind us that money didn't grow on trees.

Although my friends and I were latchkey kids residing in the same middle-class neighborhood, our family units, incomes, activities, and responsibilities were worlds apart. To say that my experience was somewhat different than my peers is an understatement. Beyond the quality of childhood toys, many of my peers attended private schools and had the resources to take family vacations, where they gained cultural experiences.

As mentioned in chapter 1, social class and economic advantages are cultural capital. Cultural experiences shape our lives, networks, and conversations. Given that people gravitate toward those who have mutual interests, I was not privy to certain circles. As a teen, I recall overhearing adults and a few neighborhood kids speak about verandas, shore excursions, and gourmet food that celebrity chefs prepared—and other terms of cultural enrichment that seemed like a foreign language. While they recollected their travel itineraries and golf outings, I worked, helping my mom, or played basketball.

If we could go back in time with the artificial intelligence we have today, we could with relative accuracy predict our future class status. The journey one takes when raised in a nuclear family with the resources to vacation with other families, golf at the country club, or take part in Van Gogh painting workshops is a journey that offers a blueprint of networks, commonalities, and refinements. If the AI algorithm continued, it would likely determine that a person with this type of journey graduated from college, had influential friends or family contacts, connected with those in positions of authority, and moved up within their company. Although this book is not about cronyism, cronyism is a common social phenomenon that grants favors or priority to personal relationships.

Favoritism occurs in all cultures. Most people have heard the phrase "It's not what you know, it's who you know." Although it's generally said with a chuckle, research shows that the adage carries considerable weight.[2] To that end, a zip code extends beyond where a person resides. It extends to the workplace and beyond. Like a zip code, a zip code story has invisible boundaries; those who live in the boundary gain preference, and those who live elsewhere are, well, out of bounds. Some may liken it to a penalty stroke in golf, but the consequences are life changers rather than game changers.

Naturally, if we succeed at work, we want to take full credit. Likewise, if we fail, we want to blame ourselves. In the corporate world, it is difficult for people to accept that their success is related to privilege, the advantage of cultural and class capital, and the opportunities that result from information and connections.

> White privilege doesn't mean your life hasn't been hard. It just means the color of your skin isn't one of the things that makes it harder.[3] —Jimmy Kimmel

KNOWLEDGE AND INFORMATION CHANGE OUR CHOICES

Some laugh at the thought of their success being caused or boosted by familial or social privilege. Some people feel it minimizes their hard work or invalidates the challenges they endured while climbing the ladder. But this is not so. Each of us makes our own choices and decisions. However, each of us makes those choices and decisions based on awareness, knowledge, and information.

I stress this point because it is difficult to process how family, culture, and economic advantage that one is born into provides opportunity and choices.[4] In this context, privilege means "the advantages that certain individuals have over others, which have been granted to them not because of what they have done but because of the social category (or categories) to which they belong."[5] Our zip code story places us in a social category. In business, advantages involve social knowledge and networks and information, which arm one with self-belief, a sense of possibility and choice, and the support needed to be aware of opportunities and the best way to act on them.

> Even the most sympathetic and insightful perspective that social science can create is obscured by what the social scientist or student cannot see, their own place in the hierarchy.[6] —Dorothy Allison

Recognizing that culture, class, and economic advantage have utility is not easy because it is simply so. It's just the way it is, so it's not something someone usually thinks about or plans. Parents, for example, condition their children. They set expectations, a sense of right and wrong, good and bad, and what is and is not appropriate. In addition, most parents teach their children how to speak, dress, stand, and address their peers and superiors. Other parents (namely those in the middle upper class and upper class) encourage, push, and even pressure their children to earn good grades. They push them to take AP classes, join school clubs, play a sport or musical instrument, get involved with extracurricular activities, or volunteer. Although parents have several good reasons for doing so, the main reason is to prepare their children to compete and thrive—rather than just survive—in college and the business world. These activities instill belief, confidence, and resilience, which set up a child for success in the business world; awareness of this is an advantage in and of itself.

Corporate business grooming usually begins in childhood. Boys are taught professional decorum and business mannerisms (particularly if they have a father living at home who works in the corporate world). It also occurs in the workplace when one male takes another under his wing. Essentially, parents prepare their children for the same life they have led and know how to lead.

That said, the idea of privilege, as in opportunity, advantage, and social membership, is not good or bad. It is just something that organizations must consider and address when planning workplace culture initiatives and mentoring or managing people from different social classes.

THE POWERFUL INFLUENCES OF SOCIAL CLASS

When people hear the term social privilege, they automatically assume the conversation has to do with race. Perhaps if you generalize it, statistically, black Americans have a higher poverty rate and thus are in a lower social class. However, what we are discussing here is not so black and white. Instead, we must analyze the powerful influences that social class exerts on one's beliefs and consciousness of social class and culture, as well as their experiences and personal and professional development. If not, diversity and inclusion in the workplace have little choice but to remain as they are.

A man is what he thinks about all day long.[7] —Ralph Waldo Emerson

The YouTube video *Life of Privilege Explained in a $100 Race* exemplifies the power that class and culture have on choices, opportunities, and chances of success.[8] Maybe more informative, the video reveals the degree of surprise or unawareness that the contestants had as to "why" they won the race—and it has nothing to do with the black race or the white race. To capture the ideas behind the "Zip Code Story," I encourage you to watch the entire four-minute video. As the eight rules of the race are presented, pay attention to the participants' faces when they are told to look back.

Now that we are past the "race card," we can begin to understand why race has been the scapegoat and why it has been grossly overly blamed for the differences, arguments, and conflicts between black and white people. Class, class bias, and culture do not simply refer to skin complexion. This construct runs deeper than skin.

New research shows that some from the middle and upper classes do not think about, are largely unaware of, and do not understand social class dynamics, revealing an unintentional implicit bias in relation to the lower social class (LSC). However, the study also reports that some in the middle class (90 percent of participants) carry "belief systems that place blame on people in LSC (e.g., people are poor because they do not work hard enough)."[9] Others in the study had similar sentiments: "if people work hard enough, they can achieve their economic goals."[10] These social beliefs perpetuate bias on the individual level, which researchers Max H. Bazerman and Don A. Moore might call "the mother of all biases,"[11] the over-confidence in the precision of our beliefs.

> Because the human mind is better at searching memory for evidence that confirms rather than disconfirms our beliefs, when we assess our confidence in a belief, it is easier for us to generate supportive rather than contradictory evidence.[12]
>   Bolstered by supportive evidence that is easily available, we overestimate the accuracy of our knowledge and the truth of our tentative hypotheses . . . this process tends to occur automatically, without conscious awareness.[13]

Bazerman and Moore also note, "Overprecision makes us too sure of our judgments, such that we are often in error yet rarely in doubt. Our assurance makes us too reluctant to take advice from others, suspicious of those whose views differ from our own, too quick to act on our opinions, and too slow to update our erroneous beliefs."[14]

As you move forward to learn more about zip codes, I would simply ask that you follow the advice of Bazerman and Moore: "consider the likelihood of alternative outcomes to the one [sic] that is familiar to you."[15] I will now break down the meaning of "zip code."

YOUR ZIP CODE AND WHAT IT MEANS

Your "zip code" and "zip code story" are not limited to where you grew up. Your story is the way you grew up, and it includes the conversations, experiences, and cultural norms that you were exposed to during your formative years.

Your zip code story involves what you experienced in your home and your community consistently. Your experiences and conversations shape the way you see and experience the world and other people. I once read that discussion around the dinner table is where children learn and adopt cultural norms and values.[16] Children who have meals with their parents tend to have higher scores and higher literacy rates. Studies show that they are also less likely to engage in risky behaviors or be pressured by drugs and premature sexual activity.

Your vocabulary, or the lack of vocabulary your parents used at home, influences how you speak and how others perceive you in public spaces. If you are taught the word "behoove," and your family and peers use it regularly, typically it becomes part of your vocabulary. In contrast, if you learn the word "behoove" in school and have a decent memory (i.e., you can spell and comprehend the word), it doesn't mean it's part of your vocabulary. The word must be a part of your daily conversations to become part of your vocabulary. If the word is not picked up through active learning, it's usually forgotten. Understanding these nuances is critical to understanding the challenges that are present when communicating with another social class.

Wealth and intelligence do not, by themselves, equal class. Social class also involves command and comprehension of particular words. Understanding why one would use such a word, then using a specific word at the appropriate time, can influence an outcome. When one is a part of the upper class, vocabulary barriers are hidden because vocabulary is part of one's upbringing. When one is not from the upper class and does not use certain words regularly, using those words may not only feel awkward, but it may also sound foreign or even peculiar to his or her social group. That said, money can only take you so far. Our zip code story shapes our vocabulary, thinking, and network. Let's look at the influences and experiences that helped shape my parents.

THE STORY OF MY PARENTS

My mother, Ella Gross, is a short, dark-brown woman who would lend her hand and home to anyone and has done so for others in need. She is chirpy and patient. She stands up for herself and her family, but she doesn't have a mean bone in her body.

My mom was brought up in the 1950s in Marianna, a rural town in north Florida. She lived in a three-bedroom home with her father, mother, and two sisters until her father died when she was seventeen years old. His death was heartbreaking and difficult on the family, but it taught my mother to be resourceful and independent at a young age. My mom was and is a hard worker. She took on side hustles such as preparing our neighbors' taxes throughout our childhood—just to make ends meet.

After high school, my mother attended a few classes at the local community college. However, expanding her education did not change the fact that Marianna could not offer her sufficient employment opportunities. After finishing her courses, my mom and her sisters moved to Jacksonville, Florida. Finding themselves in the same predicament, they packed up and moved to Washington, D.C., then finally settled in Maryland.

My father, John Gross, was six feet, one inch with a light brown complexion. Many describe him as stoic; he often reminded me of "The Thinker," as he always seemed to be in deep contemplation. An only child, dad grew up in rural Indian Head, Maryland, located in Charles County. Abandoned by his mother and grandmother as a boy, he was raised by his great-grandparents in a small two-story house that provided shelter but lacked basic amenities. They were also isolated from the social world given the absence of a telephone and television.

When it was time to take a bath or wash dishes, he had to go outside and pump water from the closest well. Until I heard this story, I never thought much about the convenience of running water. I cannot imagine carrying buckets of water several times a day, let alone in the bitter cold of winter. On top of that, when it was time to cook, my father had to chop wood to fuel the wood stove. Beyond financial hardship and emotional trauma from his mother's neglect, my dad also spoke of his experiences with racism and segregated schools.

Once you got him to open up, my dad's stories flowed like a folk song. His great-grandfather was a laborer for the federal government; his great-grandmother, a housekeeper. Each had a fourth-grade education—both had to forgo schooling to work and support the family.

Even though my dad had a difficult life, his face lit up when he spoke of the years that he played football in high school. Although no one showed up at his football games or his high-school graduation, it didn't bother him—his great-grandparents had to be proud of him, especially given the constraints placed on their education. My dad said empty bleachers at the games were an everyday experience for kids in his neighborhood. In those days, transportation, money, and parenting acumen seemed to be scarce. Plus, attendance at your child's event or being an active parent was not the social norm.

My dad wasn't big on receiving gifts, which made sense given his hardships and that he had not received gifts as a child, including Christmas gifts from his great-grandparents and other family members. As a boy, I remember asking my dad for a new pair of shoes because one of my shoes had a hole in its sole. He looked at me and, without hesitation, said, "You have a few more months of wear out of those shoes."[17] I almost didn't believe him because he always had a dry sense of humor. In later years, I realized that he was frugal because of the adversity he had faced.

Shortly after graduating high school, my father enlisted in the army—one of the only ways for him to pursue a better life, he believed. He did exceedingly well on the military aptitude test. His high scores opened the gates to the prestigious West Point Military Academy.

Although he was nominated for his superior grade point average (GPA), character, and physical fitness, my father could not think about moving forward. My father and his great-grandparents were more concerned about food and safety needs.[18] My father admitted that he passed up the opportunity to be a cadet because his focus was on obtaining "realistic" work. In those days, he had no room for dreams. He knew a surefire way to bring home food and ensure safety, so if he had any dreams of being groomed to be an officer, they were superseded by survival needs. He also said that his great-grandparents, given their limited education, did not understand the long-term value of attending the academy. Instead, my father served in the army. He was trained in telephone transmission repair, which he leveraged once he became a civilian, eventually landing a job in Maryland with the federal government.

My parents met on the job at the Indian Head Naval Surface Warfare Center in Maryland. In 1978, they settled in Fort Washington, Maryland. My sister, Selina, was born shortly after. I was born two years later. Coming from a rural survivalist upbringing, on the surface my parents appeared to hold similar values. But my mother wanted more from life than my father, which was a source of friction in their relationship.

My mom wanted the American dream. She wanted to marry, own a house, and maybe own a business one day. On the other hand, my dad disliked being tied down to a relationship and did not want the responsibility of home ownership—hard to blame him knowing the grueling labor that went into supporting his parents and their home.

When I was three years old, my dad moved out. Although he no longer lived in our house, he came by frequently and spent time with Selina and me doing activities that he had planned for us. My parents seemed to work out their differences to ensure that Selina and I were properly cared for—they never put us in the middle or made us think that the other parent didn't love us. This experience helped me in a future downfall.

While working, maintaining a household, and caring for two children was taxing for my mom, she knew how to handle difficult situations and get results under pressure. Because my mom was friendly and always lent a hand to neighbors, she had built a trusting network of people who were happy to care for Selina and me while she was at work.

Before separating, my parents had rented a three-bedroom single-family rancher located across the street from a recreational park and Baptist church, which Mom made sure we attended regularly. Although our home was not small, it was modest compared to our neighbors' homes.

As a teenager, I took a paper route. It allowed me to see the inside of the houses in my neighborhood. Some had pools, koi ponds, huge yards, and three-car garages. One had an elevator. One of my neighbors played for the Washington Bullets, a professional National Basketball Association team. I didn't meet most of the kids in our neighborhood until middle school or high school because they attended private schools, and I attended local public schools. Crime and drugs were present in our community, though not unchecked.

Although my sister and I grew up in Fort Washington, one of the most affluent African American communities in the country, we did not feel affluent because our home only had one parent and, for the most part, one income. Compared to our neighbors, we did not take the same types of family trips, wear the same clothing, or have the same conversations. And our parents had different expectations. We always had an older model car; Selina and I would kind of sink into the seats so the neighbors wouldn't see us. Although I was not aware of social class at the time, I recall a few distinct memories that made me feel like my friends were different from me. For example, one Christmas, I remember showing off my remote-control car to a friend. Then he showed me his new robot. The robot not only stood as tall as he did but was cutting-edge technology at that time.

Another friend received a brand new three-wheel dirt bike. One summer day, he and I went for a ride along a dirt trail where National Harbor would one day stand along the Potomac. Only I was riding a secondhand minibike. I could barely keep pace—then, without warning, my bike snapped in two. I crashed to the ground as the front wheel and handlebars detached from the frame. I was not seriously injured, but I did realize my bike was seriously inferior to my friend's.

As I got older, I noticed differences beyond just money and material things. I began to see differences in household rules, routines, and parenting approaches. My friends' parents spoke to them about the importance of education, relationships, and setting goals. Many had curfews and could not play outside after dark. When the streetlights came on, the neighborhood turned into a ghost town. Some were in JROTC, the Junior Reserve Officer Training Corps, where they learned leadership skills; others focused on education.

Most of my friends played sports in high school. Their parents encouraged and sometimes forced them to get involved because teamwork builds character, teaches self-discipline, and enriches communication skills.

I once asked my dad if I could join the football team, but he discouraged me. At the time, it didn't take much because I was more concerned about making a buck to buy the clothing and sneakers that my friends wore. Unlike my friends, I didn't see the value in playing sports. No one brought it up, but I remember thinking that sports had no immediate payoff.

Like many teenagers whose parents could not afford to buy us the latest fashions, concert tickets, or the coolest electronics gadgets, I worked. Work was more important to me than school because I could see an immediate return. The idea of playing sports or going to college was not really in my field of vision. Given my parents' knowledge and experience, they did not suggest that I join a school sports team or club or attempt to further my education because they could not see the future benefits. Meanwhile, some of my friends had built character and discipline because they worked, focused on academics, and played a sport. In those days, education was not my strongest suit.

LEARNING STRUGGLES

When I was a child, I hated school. I struggled to understand the concepts, and I dreaded being called on to read out loud. In class, sweat would bead my forehead just anticipating the teacher calling on me to read. Every student stumbled while reading passages, but I bombed entire excerpts because I could not decode words quickly.

No matter how hard I tried, the letters on the page seemed to move around like they had tiny feet under them. The challenge I faced at school made me lose interest in education. My mom hired private tutors and took me to different reading programs to help me learn, but nothing helped.

As a result of dyslexia, I distanced myself from everything that had to do with education. As a teenager, I recall saying things backward. My friends laughed but thankfully did not mock me too much because I played it like it was intentional, like I was doing word tricks. It was embarrassing. Because of struggles that my learning disability caused, I believed college was out of the question for me, and no one encouraged me to think otherwise, likely the case for other class migrants.

During my junior and senior years in high school, I took a drafting class taught by a veteran mechanical designer. He showed the class photos of his cars and the high-profile projects that he had designed. He also bragged that he earned large sums of money without having earned a college degree. That was all the confirmation I needed.

After high school, I enrolled in the Maryland Drafting Institute, an architectural, civil, and mechanical drafting trade school. Tyree, a close family relation and my first mentor, was a mechanical engineer. At the time, I admired him because he was smart, had a cool car, and took care of his wife. Once I learned that he worked on submarines, I was sold and decided to follow in his footsteps.

I excelled in mechanics because drafting had little to do with reading and writing and more to do with shapes, mathematics, and how things work. Dyslexia became an advantage for understanding architectural, mechanical, three-dimensional drawings, and mechanical calculations. Much later, I realized that people with dyslexia possess unique talents and abilities. The book *The Gift of Dyslexia: Why Some of the Smartest People Can't Read and How They Can Learn*, written by Ronald D. Davis and Eldon M. Braun, taught me that people with dyslexia are endowed with the ability to engage in disassociation.[19] Disassociation allows people with dyslexia to mentally detach from an object and create three dimensional models in their minds. For example, if I were to look at a two-dimensional drawing of a cup, my brain could visualize the cup in three dominions. That is, I can rotate images in my mind and mentally see the cup from different angles.

This skill was advantageous in drafting and engineering because it allowed me to process problems and find solutions efficiently. I was able to run calculations in my head, which helped me size mechanical ductwork by merely looking at a drawing and taking in some preliminary numbers. I was able to see how things operated and fit together in my head and then apply it to a drawing. I experienced job security and opportunities for upward mobility in engineering because I had built some self-confidence, which made me open, eager, and willing to be coached.

Years later, I realized that disassociation could also apply to complex business system problems and interpersonal relationship problems. My innate abilities to understand complex mechanical, business, and relationship challenges helped me change my career and become a serious player in the consulting world.

The benefits of dyslexia were limited. Although dyslexia helped me in engineering, I still struggled with self-doubt and the fear of not being smart enough. On top of this, throughout my youth and until I was diagnosed, my parents knew little about dyslexia and thus had no idea what to do. They did not know how to find help, support, or speak with me about the shame and guilt that had followed me into adulthood. And because I didn't understand dyslexia or realize that it was actually an advantage, I was ashamed and kept it hidden from everyone.

By my mid-twenties, based on things I had heard, I assumed that I had dyslexia. Still, it was not confirmed until I visited the Maryland Division of Rehabilitation Services. Here, at the age of thirty, I was officially diagnosed.

Up to this point, most of my life decisions were rooted in fear— thinking I was not smart enough and that I could not learn. Until my diagnosis, I was unaware that support was available at the college level. By this time, I was married and in my early thirties; and although I was good at engineering, I had grown tired of working in the field. Frankly, drawing lines and shapes all day and performing calculations bored the heck out of me. At the same time, I had an insatiable thirst to connect with people and help them on a more personal level.

While pursuing my bachelor's degree, life as I knew it began to fall apart. Returning to college took a toll on me and my marriage. I worked two jobs to make ends meet, which were both heavy administrative positions that required considerable reading and writing. Not only was my employment always hanging in the balance because dyslexia prevented me from keeping pace with the workload, but my wife and I divorced because of all the stress and strain.

HOW MY ZIP CODE STORY CAME INTO PLAY

After I graduated from college, I met many well-educated, successful people who had dyslexia and learned how to manage it. Our zip code story was the chief difference between us. One colleague, Heather Kaye, had grown up in an affluent area near Washington, D.C. She was diagnosed with dyslexia early and sent to a school that offered special education services for students with learning disabilities. Heather went on to earn her master's degree and is the founder and CEO of InVision LLC, a leadership consulting firm. When we shared our stories, I remember her saying, "If you live[d] in a different zip code, you would have received better learning supports at school, like myself."[20] Heather's success was not because she was white. Instead, her zip code, family support, educational resources, early detection and intervention played key roles in her story.

John H. Cammack, a former senior executive with T. Rowe Price, told me that both he and his father had dyslexia. His advice was impactful and memorable. He told me his father was a successful business owner who said that learning would be difficult at an early age, but he would be uniquely advantaged when it came to problem solving.[21] Because John's dad was both dyslexic and successful, he coached his son through the obstacles and learning challenges that John faced while achieving his college degree. He later helped John navigate and land a high-level position at T. Rowe Price. Over the years, I've heard numerous success stories about people who have dyslexia, including Richard Branson, Tom Cruise, Leonardo da Vinci, Walt Disney, Jim Carrey, Albert Einstein, Whoopi Goldberg, John F. Kennedy, George Washington, George W. Bush, and a host of other well-known people. It didn't happen overnight, but once I believed that I could be successful (even with dyslexia), my life began to change.

I didn't view dyslexia as a gift; to me, it was a curse, a life sentence to low-paying, dead-end jobs. Although I grew up in a nice neighborhood with a decent education system, my zip code story did not support my learning disability, confidence, or belief in myself. My zip code story consisted of more than just my physical surroundings; it entailed the conversations that my parents both had and didn't have with me. My parents passed down and passed on everything they could; unfortunately, their self-doubt and self-limiting beliefs were passed on, too.

My parents' success and their lack thereof shaped my possibilities and horizons in life. This is the most significant nuance in a physical zip code versus a figurative zip code, which I call the zip code story. You can be brought up in the worst neighborhood in America but have parents who strive for more and feed you positive information. Or you can grow up in an area with plenty of opportunities and resources but not believe in yourself, so you don't have the confidence needed to access the information or resources. Both zip codes stories can lead to a particular social class or type of life, whether or not you want it.

As a manager or your own leader, it's essential to become more aware of your zip code story and that of others. It can determine your outlook on life, expand your leadership skills, and enhance your internal and external conversation.

DECISION MAKING AND MISSED OPPORTUNITIES

Like most people, I've made plenty of decisions, good and bad. However, I've also missed out on some important opportunities because of my zip code story. As mentioned earlier in this chapter, based on my knowledge, support, and circumstances as a teenager, I decided to pursue a trade school instead of college. Some twenty years later, I attended college to earn a bachelor's degree; now, in 2021, I am working toward my master's degree.

The point is, our zip code story can influence or limit our social class—sometimes for the rest of our lives. I could have begun building toward my future at an earlier age if I had had the insights, belief, and support.

Going to college straight after high-school graduation would not only have better prepared me for the business world, but it would also have shown me different possibilities and helped me make gainful career choices. Although I would have continued to struggle in school because of dyslexia, most colleges (as I have since learned) would have supported me and my efforts to obtain a degree. But I am thankful for the skills I honed at the trade school, which allowed me to become a mechanical designer, helped me to develop self-confidence, and eventually set me on a path that revealed my calling.

Although education is not the only class component, it can be a major one in certain environments. For instance, in 2015, I was surprised to learn that "College graduates, on average, earned 56% more than high school grads."[22]

Although I was eager to earn money in high school, I wish my parents had pushed me to play football. I thought that my father would have encouraged it because he played football. Instead, he discouraged me because he wanted to protect me from injury and failed to see the positive influence it could have on my future.

I do not blame myself or my parents for their lack of judgment or insight. I've learned that most people are bound by their own awareness and life experiences. Of course, my parents were also bound by lack of education and access to information (i.e., lack of guidance from their parents, the internet, and social circles).

The parents in our neighborhood didn't push their children to play a sport for no reason. Playing sports develops self-esteem, discipline, competitiveness, and teamwork. Many companies look for these attributes when hiring entry-level sales associates and first-line managers, and they are necessary to be successful in business in general.

Instead of sports, I worked part-time at a fast-food restaurant, which gave me sales and customer service experience. Unfortunately, working at an early age to earn and spend money on my immediate needs set a precedent for how I would live, spend, and save for a decade and a half after high school, well into my thirties.

After deciding to attend college, I was offered a scholarship to Prince George's Community College, which could have led to a scholarship at the University of Maryland if I could maintain the GPA requirements. Again, I did not have the confidence, belief, support, or fortitude necessary to pursue this opportunity. I also believed that it was impossible to attend school full-time because I would only be able to work part-time—leaving me short $800–$1,000 each month. Between fear, monetary concerns, and reading issues, all I could see was a wall of obstacles, so I dismissed the opportunity.

One year later, I bumped into a guy I had met at a professional training seminar in 2010. I asked what he was doing in the library. He told me that he had to get out of the house; he needed a quiet place to study for his bachelor's degree, which was facilitated through an entrepreneurial scholarship at the local community college. As he shared more about the program, I realized that he was enrolled in the program I had chosen not to pursue. I interrupted him to say that I had received an offer for admission to the same program but could not make it happen on a part-time salary. He said, "Oh, you didn't know about the stipend?"[23] My jaw dropped. "Stipend?" I asked. If I had had the self-belief, had known that colleges offer support services and that all I had to do was complete some forms to receive an $800 stipend each month, my coaching career likely would have started earlier.

Years later, I told my teenage daughter the "stipend" story as she was contemplating college. It was vital for her to realize that intelligence and finances have little or nothing to do with why people go to college and complete their degrees. Instead, striving for that degree has everything to do with their desire, self-belief, support network, and the mentorship they receive. Combined, this translates to their zip code story.

My zip code story was not all bad. I could have made worse decisions, particularly in my high-school days when I was looking to earn extra cash. One time a schoolmate, who lived in an adjacent neighborhood, approached me with an opportunity to sell drugs.

For a minute, I considered the offer because I was excited about the idea of making a quick buck. Fortunately, I didn't know anyone who sold or used drugs. Plus, I think it helped to see both of my parents go to work and play by the rules, so selling drugs and the risk of serving time in prison were not in my field of vision or part of my zip code story.

My zip code story began to change through personal development, relationships, mentorships, and other illuminating experiences. I started to see possibilities and developed a desire to achieve more personally and professionally. Changing my zip code story opened the door to several opportunities and achievements over the years. These included writing my first book, *Seeds of Greatness*; earning my coaching certification and my bachelor's degree in organizational management; and learning how to skydive, scuba dive, speak Spanish, and other accomplishments, which I will share in later chapters. By far, my most significant achievement was pursuing my purpose in life: inspiring and motivating others. Although we should not question our purpose, I believe my goals would have been reached sooner had I had guidance at a younger age.

LIVING BETWEEN ZIP CODES

Studies show that the average person stops making friends at age twenty-five.[24] This happens for several reasons, but mainly because it's challenging to form close relationships as an adult, particularly when working and raising a family. In general, relationships already established by adulthood are more comfortable and easier to maintain than developing new ones. Comfort zones are cozy, but they stunt our growth.

I grew up with some great friends. Although we lived in the same neighborhood, we had different zip code stories. Learning more about them and their families allowed me to expand my story. Unfortunately, though, their zip code stories were limited, too, because we lived in a predominantly African American community. It had little diversity, which meant that everyone in our zip code had an African American frame of reference.

Some of my neighborhood friends attended private schools, and some went on family trips. Still, I don't recall hearing about skiing trips, hiking or skeet shooting, which at one time were unusual activities for African Americans. It was not that families in my neighborhood did not have the financial resources to experience different types of activities because they did go on vacations and take part in other activities that far exceeded my experiences. But some things were just not a part of their zip code story.

As I got older, this became a problem. Each time I tried something new or different, my friends and family looked at me like I was from Mars. In 2009, when my friends found out that I went skydiving, their eyebrows froze in shock. Two years later, they looked at me with those same disbelief upon my return from a firewalking event that Tony Robbins had held at Long Beach, California—being frowned upon kind of curbed my enthusiasm. I recall feeling dispirited that I had no one to share my happiness with nor anyone to recognize the courage it took for me to step out of my comfort zone to try something new. But that didn't stop me. In 2012, I attended a pig race; a year later, I really shook up things at home and on the mountaintops when I went snowboarding. It was intimidating because I didn't see any other African Americans skiing in the Poconos. I kept most of these tales to myself, figuring that I'd get kicked out of my community if I continued to press my luck.

Some of these were not expensive activities—they just weren't the kind of activities that matched their zip code story. And although we lived in the same zip code, my interests, activities, and conversations didn't quite fit into either world.

From this point, it became apparent to me that figuratively I was living between zip codes. As I leaned toward a new zip code story, I outgrew my old zip code and story. For years, I found myself holding back my ideas and passions in both circles. The combination of awkwardness and feeling as though I didn't belong or fit comfortably in either zip code was disheartening. I felt a sense of dissonance and self-doubt no matter which direction I turned.

As I socialized and mingled with new colleagues and coworkers in the middle upper class, I still felt uncomfortable. Holding a conversation was laborious and painful at times, even though we did have some activities in common.

WHY CLASS MIGRANTS FEEL OUT OF PLACE

I am not alone. Many class migrants who are between zip codes face the same harsh realities. They experience internal conflict and self-doubts along with the daily grind and challenges that both work and life present. I can imagine it being similar to the way my father felt when he returned from the military. Kind of disoriented, out of touch—like his old story, life, and identity weren't relevant or applicable to who he had become.

Feeling out of place has been an ongoing theme in my life. When I was a mechanical designer, I worked at a job site on K Street in Washington, D.C. It was a remarkably diverse company, which brought a comfort level that differed from the rest—that is, until one of my coworkers brought up a recent vacation that he had taken and compared it to other places he traveled to in the past in Europe, Asia, and Australia. Another colleague chimed in about her experience touring Africa. When my turn to share came, all I could say was I spent a lot of time visiting my great aunt in Jacksonville, Florida. The conversation ended in awkward silence.

Class migrants frequently find themselves caught in the crossfire. I call it a clash of zip code stories. When your background limits your experiences, you will likely find yourself unable to contribute to the conversation in a meaningful way. These situations can be confusing, frustrating, and embarrassing for the class migrant and all parties involved. Zip code clashes are likely the top reason migrants gravitate toward their native zip codes—preventing them from forging new connections and networks with people from other social classes.

Vulnerability and authenticity are the main ingredients involved in developing trust in new relationships. However, they are two of the most challenging attributes for the class migrant to maintain. Class migrants must crawl out on a limb to overcome the fear of rejection.

Expectations in the corporate world can create even more confusion. La Juan Carter is one class migrant who used the power of authenticity to drive her career. She grew up in Washington, D.C., and rose through the ranks of corporate America by keeping sight of who she is and how that benefits the trusting relationships she builds. Maintaining a sense of self help La Juan overcame racial and class barriers. The "what you see is what you get" is not an attitude but a way of accepting and being true to herself. La Juan is aware of social class, but she never let it get in her way. Her strength lies in her integrity to be genuine, and it's responsible for her successful career and role as a director of contracts.

> Maybe I did not speak the language, maybe I did not have the background, but I had wisdom from where and how I grew up. There was something valuable there that, regardless of my social class, it helped propel me. But also, I had to have the drive and determination to make it no matter what.
>
> Because I felt like I always wanted to represent the most authentic version of me I possibly could, I didn't want to be Sally. I don't want to be Karen; I don't want to be the Asian version of La Juan; I just want to be La Juan Carter from Washington, D.C. That La Juan comes in many different forms and shapes. So, sometimes I have to make sure that I don't compromise on my authentic version of who I want to be just to appease a group of people who don't look like me. This can be challenging for those who come from backgrounds similar to mine.

I certainly believe that you can be marginalized and alienated in some way just because of your choices. The people who do that do not understand the nature or the mindset of the individual being alienated. But you have to learn how to navigate those troubled waters because it's there. It's always going to present itself, and that's where you have to take control of your own destiny and decide how you are going to handle the situation; how are you going to beat this bigoted individual who believes that they are the author of your destiny because you think differently. You have to know how to navigate these situations without allowing them to taint your motivation.

If you compromise your integrity of who you are, you become a shape-shifter, in my opinion. Ultimately, people are going to lose respect for you because you can only shape-shift and hide who you are for so long. At some point, you are going to get caught. It's the law of the universe. There are certain laws of the universe that are always going to be there no matter what you are doing, personally or professionally. At the end of the day, people respect an authentic person; they respect people who they can trust. (La Juan Carter, interview by author, "How one class migrant used the power of authenticity to drive her career," n.d.)

Authenticity can be a challenge for class migrants in the corporate world because they must balance the authentic self in a workplace environment that can feel unauthentic. There is also the desire to fit in, be liked, and follow office etiquette, which can cause uncertainty for the class migrant who strives to be authentic. Those desires usually don't come naturally for people in a new environment and require personal and professional risk. Along with these risks and unknowns, class migrants face social pressures and stereotypes that bring about an uncomfortable awareness. Being aware is usually a good thing, but it can make class migrants question their self-presentation when being "real" or engaging from a genuine place. La Juan makes a conscious effort not to compromise her authenticity because she knows it's a fool's errand. Class migrants must navigate these uncharted territories and create a new but authentic work identity that comprises their ideas, beliefs, and values. I want to note that authenticity is not about clothing or style—those are choices external to a person's core beliefs and attributes.

Ultimately, everybody puts on a front to suit the occasion. Most people will prepare themselves differently for work than for a night at the movies. Putting on a front can be a challenge for class migrants because they are not preparing for a two-hour film; they must prepare for a different culture. Doing so is taxing because it often requires them to play a new role and suppress part of their true identity while creating a new authentic identity for the corporate office. At the same time, with little to no social support at work, they must learn the unspoken rules, norms, and customs of the white-collar setting to fit in, be seen for merits over embodied status, and gain acceptance by the majority culture.

On the one hand, as class migrants embark on a journey of growth and transformation, they need to rely on those unique relationships, new and old, that encourage, support, and nourish and give them a sense of belonging. On the other hand, familiar relationships can hold back class migrants. Friends and even family can show signs of disapproval when migrants break the image they are expected to be—similar to the experience I had with my friends when I took up skiing.

It's also easier to keep the same relationships because it involves less risk. That is, you do not have to make yourself vulnerable or struggle with the idea of being authentic or being seen as inauthentic. It is challenging to be authentic when you are in a new environment, and you're still learning the ropes that everyone else seems to have a command of, such as the business protocols and norms.

Complacency offers contentment. We can only grow by placing ourselves in new situations. Said another way, new situations make us uncomfortable, but that's where growth occurs. Building new relationships is key to developing support, learning new customs, and finding new mentorships, which have helped me most in my personal and professional life.

> Challenge yourself; it's the only path which leads to growth.[25]
> —Morgan Freeman

LEARNING HOW TO BELIEVE IN YOURSELF

In my late twenties, I met my second mentor, Bob Baker. He founded an insurance company, and he was all about personal development. This mentorship gave me space and encouragement to open my mind further, change my zip code story, and debunk my old beliefs and start healthier new ones. Bob and I frequently met for coffee to discuss my goals and the future life I saw for myself. He recommended that I study a few books and audio programs. One audio program that changed my thinking was *The Strangest Secret* by Earl Nightingale.[26]

The audiobook by Nightingale reminded me of Reginald F. Lewis. I spoke about Lewis in chapter 1. He was a Harvard grad with a juris doctorate who established the first African American Wall Street law firm. His parents had the insight and wherewithal to support and encourage him, but equally crucial to Lewis's success was his ability to have a settled purpose, a firm belief or certainty of accomplishment in his mind. Lewis's two daughters and his half-brother, Jean S. Fugett Jr., former all-star for the Dallas Cowboys and Washington Redskins, made their dreams come true because they believed anything was possible. They believed that if you imagine, believe in yourself, work hard, and seek ways to make a difference, you will.

I've learned that once you hone self-belief, you won't succumb to failure or fears of attempting the unknown. In fact, under your self-guided belief, any potential failure is processed as a learning experience that only strengthens knowledge. Self-belief doesn't come naturally for all of us; otherwise, everyone would be successful. Of all the awkward moments and personal challenges that I've faced, self-belief was the most challenging hurdle, but the hurdle with the largest payout. It takes a lifetime to program our minds with beliefs. Yet, it only took me three months to debunk the ones that no longer served me. I was able to purge my negative self-beliefs and reprogram the beliefs required to be open to opportunities, take chances, and find my purpose.

We become what we think about.[27] —Earl Nightingale

Bob Baker could not have steered me in a better direction. He invited me to meetings and introduced me to his colleagues and clients. Bob showed me how he operated his business —offering me the skeleton key to success in any industry. I also had an opportunity to see how he functioned around his wife. I took it all in. This was the first time I had ever been out with someone who owned a successful business. Since that time, I have had several mentors, coaches, and friendships that helped me expand my zip code story. Without those influential and pivotal relationships, you might not be reading this book right now. I can admit that those relationships gave me certain privileges, helped me uncover new possibilities, and changed my life and career trajectory for the better.

LEARNING EMPATHY BY WALKING
IN SOMEONE ELSE'S SHOES

I became a single parent after my divorce, primarily because I lived in a better school district than my ex-wife. This part of my zip code story was one of the most challenging experiences in my life, but it helped me develop emotional intelligence. I have two daughters: Christen and Lauren. Now 21 and 23 years old, respectively, they were around 7 and 9 years old at the time of the divorce. I learned quickly; being a single parent meant lots of responsibility, lots of stress, and lots of coordinating school events, play dates, birthday parties, hair appointments, movie nights, and doctor's appointments. Single parenting was highly challenging for me because during this time I attended college, wrote a book, and started a business, all while working a regular job. At one point, I started incorporating my daughters into my businesses.

I was always doing odd jobs in my youth to make extra money, so entrepreneurship never felt too intimidating. When I owned a vending machine business, my oldest daughter helped me restock the snacks. When I started my speaking business, both daughters sold books and T-shirts at the back of the room. Initially, I didn't want to involve the kids because I thought they would be in the way. It turned out to be a great learning experience for all of us. I sold more merchandise, and they received valuable work experience. My oldest daughter, Christen, capitalized on these experiences, which helped her land her first job at the International Spy Museum in Washington, D.C.

I share this part of my zip code story because it's essential to realize that it wasn't all a bed of roses. In fact, it was more weeds than roses. I had to force myself to overcome many challenges and conflicts. For example, I worked as a community engagement coordinator for a well-known nonprofit organization in Washington, D.C. I was responsible for running the day-to-day operations of the Community Engagement Department, managing six staff members and coordinating multiple events across the city. The average morning looked something like this: up at 5:30 a.m., dress the girls, drive across town, drop them off at school, and then arrive at work to facilitate my staff meetings. After an exhausting workday canvassing the community and talking with community members and constituents, I sprinted across town in rush-hour traffic to pick up the girls by 6:30 p.m. They did their homework in the car on the way home, and I checked it once we got home, in between making dinner.

Just writing these words makes me tired all over again. But this was my routine. If you have ever watched the movie *The Pursuit of Happiness*,[28] you know a bit about my story. My ex-wife helped and did her part, but I knew that she could only do so much from a different household. These experiences turned out to be highly instrumental for me. Even though my mother was a single mom, I could not understand her actual struggles and dilemmas—and she did her best to hide any signs of stress around my sister and me. Having to experience the trials and tribulations of single parenting myself really sank in. It later helped me relate to single parents I coached and worked with throughout my consulting career. As mentioned in chapter 1, understanding what someone likes is vital to understanding how to help them accomplish their goals. When you show compassion or empathy for their pain points, the relationship and insights go much further.

PERSONAL DEVELOPMENT

Above all, as I reflect on my journey, personal development has helped me the most in life. It helped me be open, believe in myself, take chances, let down my guard (show vulnerability), and remain authentic. It's even responsible for accelerating my personal growth because it helped me change my zip code. Subsequently, I developed a new zip code story.

Personal development includes working on yourself mentally, emotionally, physically, spiritually, financially, and personally through different modalities. I have engaged and continue to engage in personal development, so much so, it's a habit. I made sure to free my schedule to have ample time to read books, watch videos, hire coaches, find mentors, attend seminars and workshops, and create vision boards. As part of this process, I also set up interviews with people who accomplished something that I desired, pursuing new experiences. I maximized my personal time by listening to audio programs in the car—at least when the girls weren't with me. Engaging in personal development helped me find a new career and life purpose, which propelled me to shift my career from mechanical engineering to author, consulting coach, and keynote speaker.

Two other personal development audio programs made an impact on my life. *I Could Do Anything If I Only Knew What It Was: How to Discover What You Really Want and How to Get It*[29] by Barbara Sher was monumental for my self-discovery. It helped me envision a crystal-clear image of what I wanted my life to look like in the future. A career in engineering was not in the picture—not even a little. Sher's book presented several questions that zeroed in on what I would like to do, what I was good at, and what I found inspiring. I did not take this lightly. I listened carefully and played by the book because I genuinely wanted to change my situation. I had no one to walk me through the steps needed to prepare myself for the future I desired. I began by using the answers that I had written down from Sher's questionnaire. Those answers helped me develop a vision statement of what I wanted my future life to look like.

The second audio program, *Goals: Setting and Achieving Them on Schedule* by Zig Ziglar,[30] assisted me in identifying specific goals that I needed to achieve (incrementally) to move my life forward. For example, I wanted to purchase a home for my family, but I didn't think I made enough money for the house I desired. After listening to the audio program, I identified some subgoals like polishing my credit, saving for the down payment, and looking for a realtor. Within a year, I had closed on my first home—in the neighborhood I had wanted to live in, and shortly after that, I bought a second car. From there, my list of goals and accomplishments started to grow exponentially.

My accomplishments included writing another book, starting a nonprofit organization, working toward my master's degree, purchasing a laundromat, and finding my way onto the local news channel. The fulfillment gained from these accomplishments hooked me on personal development.

Today, I experience a variety of personal development modalities such as meditation, mindfulness, and even swimming. Yes, that's right. I consider swimming a form of personal development. It's physical development and spiritual development all in one. After swimming forty laps (not to be confused with Olympic laps), I feel a sense of peace and calm but also alertness. It may be difficult to understand if you're not a swimmer, but it feels renewing and revitalizing. Swimming wasn't a big part of my childhood, but swimming laps became a goal of mine, which now, through personal development, is a part of my zip code story. I've also expanded my religious and spiritual zip code by attending a Christian church and a spiritual center, which helps me apply biblical principles to work and life.

I have taken the scenic route to success. But through my education, personal experiences, professional reflections, and insights as a leadership coach, I have put together questions designed to help class migrants envision their goals and lay out their first blueprint for success. At the same time, the questions help managers and human resources practitioners see how their zip code story may compare to mine or another class migrant at work. My work in the inclusion, diversity, equity, accessibility (IDEA) space has helped me create questions that serve class migrants and management in the workplace. The people who take the time to finish these questions and reflect on them will get the most out of this process. Enjoy the experience of learning.

3

What's Your Zip Code Story?

Just imagine for a day that you do not know anything, that what you believe could be completely false. Let go of your preconceptions and even your most cherished beliefs. Experiment. Force yourself to hold the opposite opinion or see the world through your enemy's eyes. Listen to the people around you with more attentiveness. See everything as a source for education—even the most banal encounters. Imagine that the world is still full of mystery. When you operate this way, you will notice that something strange often happens. Opportunities will begin to fall into your lap because you are suddenly more receptive to them. Sometimes luck or serendipity is more a function of the openness of your mind.[1] —50 Cent and Robert Greene, *The 50th Law*

Whether you're a class migrant, recruiting manager, or manager, it is important to understand your zip code story. It shapes your perspective and how you engage with people in your professional and personal life.

Understanding your zip code story can reveal your blind spots and help you navigate any barriers you have created so you can form new bridges. For example, you may not know why you treat one employee or friend better than the other, but maybe you have a better connection because you share a similar zip code story.

If you've never thought about your zip code story until now, you likely have not considered the role your experiences, cultural nuances, travel, and educational achievements have played in your blind spots, biases, and preferences.

I have prepared some questions to help you reflect on your zip code story. To get the most out of these questions, find a quiet place and carve out some time for deep contemplation. Once you have more clarity on your zip code story, you will see class bias with 20/20 vision.

Below are eight questions and summaries that help you look deeper at your zip code story. For each question, ask yourself these follow-ups:

- How did the answer affect how you see the world now?
- How did the answer make you feel as a child?
- What memories did the questions arouse?

1.   Describe where you grew up (i.e., home and neighborhood).
In my 2021 TEDx RushU Talk, I opened my session by asking the audience, "What would you think if I told you I lived in the Beverly Hills 90210 zip code? Would you think that I grew up in a nice neighborhood, attended a prestigious college, or was well traveled? Would you think that I did not have to work hard for what I got in life?"

I asked these questions to help viewers connect to the place they grew up and get them to think about how they or others may perceive them. In my talk, I go on to share that your zip code story is not just about *where* you grew up; it's about *how* you grew up. So, for this section, I want you to think about your neighborhood.

When I was a kid growing up in Fort Washington, Maryland, Halloween was a big deal. Everyone in our neighborhood participated. I lived across the street from a Baptist church, and even it put on Halloween events that included a haunted house, apple bobbing, costume parties, and contests. Frankly, I am surprised that our community church participated in Halloween rituals.

As Halloween approached, our neighbors would adorn their homes with glowing pumpkins, skeletons, and fake spiders hanging on cobwebs. Some went to great lengths to construct coffins with fake mummies that popped out every fifteen or twenty minutes. To say that my neighbors liked Halloween is an understatement.

The kids in our neighborhood knew which house had the best candy. My friends and I never had formal plans, but we did have a strategy for trick-or-treating. Unbeknownst to us, our trick-or-treating preferences hinged on past experiences and biases. First, we determined the size of the houses and their location, then used this information to plot our trick-or-treat route for the evening. We started with the bigger homes because they gave out the best candy.

Trick-or-treating was one of my favorite pastimes as a child. The entire neighborhood came together as one to celebrate this holiday. Writing this book made me realize how much my community impacted me and the profound meaning of my zip code story. My neighborhood gave me a sense of belonging, safety, and feeling heard and understood. My strong sense of community shaped my purpose, my thoughts, and my engagements.

Bringing people together has always been a priority to me. Whether it's a holiday, college campus rally, or sporting event, people make connections, and those connections form communities.

- How did your childhood community and experiences shape your zip code story?
- Did you move often?
- Did your family reside in a large house, modest house, or an apartment?
- Did you know your neighbors well?
- Did you like your neighbors?
- Did you grow up in a rural area, urban city, near the coast, on a farm, in a mobile home, or maybe on a boat?
- Did you spend some of your childhood living with different relatives or attending boarding school?

The experiences from your formative years have shaped your preferences, biases, and beliefs.

During a training workshop focused on inclusive work cultures, Brandan, a colleague at Cook Ross, mentioned that he moved multiple times because he was a "military brat"—the child of a parent who serves full-time in the military, wherein the family must relocate upon military request. To survive this lifestyle or uprooting, he said he learned how to make friends quickly. Moving can be an unsettling experience, even as an adult. In his case, relocations were challenging because they typically occurred in the middle of the school year, so his peers had already established friend groups, relationships, and cliques at school and in his new neighborhood. As he matured, he explained, he instinctively learned how to adapt to his new environment. As a result, he became resourceful and developed keen social skills that allowed him to fit in, make friends, and gain group acceptance, which helped him navigate the rules, customs, and norms in his new environment.

These tools are helpful for class migrants in the workplace. Feeling connected, accepted, and belonging is essential to every human, which I'll discuss in chapter 7.

Who we are is deeply rooted in our formative years (i.e., the house we grew up in, those we interacted with, the memories of the physical environment, and how that environment made us feel).

We often assume that others have the same philosophies, beliefs, and knowledge. But they don't. When we fail to expand our zip code story, we subconsciously take our experiences, memories, and perspectives and project them onto others, both personally and professionally. Expecting others to have the same beliefs, behavior, and common sense as yourself can cause unintentional insults and barriers to relationships that would benefit both parties.

Without awareness, intention, or control, we may try to reinvent our experience. When we are oblivious to how our history influences our decision making, we can quickly become stuck in a reenactment of our past or develop destructive behaviors in an attempt to forget about the past. Consequently, people may do things such as purchase a house beyond their means or judge others who have not had their experience or have had "in their eyes" a better experience.

Several years ago, I was looking to purchase a new house, but I kept looking at one-story ranch houses. Finally, my fiancée asked, "Why do you keep looking at these one-story flats? They look like ranches." I responded, "I know. Cool, right?" My partner replied, "No, not cool at all."

On the other hand, my partner would always choose houses with columns on the front entrance. She said columns reminded her of royalty. I didn't see it. We searched for both ranches and homes with columns because these were the type of houses we grew up in, and we wanted to re-create them even if they didn't fit our budget or exact needs. Our zip code stories drive us because we internalize the values and norms that we are familiar with and learned while growing up. How does your zip code story show up in your personal or professional life?

2. Name some social and cultural norms in your childhood environment.

Cultural or social norms could include but are not limited to eating around the dinner table, using profanity, playing family games, watching television shows, and so on. Social scientists say social norms are a part of our culture.[2] Social norms drive us more than any other influence in our lives. Most of the conflicts I see in companies and our personal lives come from the differences in a person's culture. I'll share a couple of examples that highlight how culture can lead to conflict.

When I was twenty-seven years old, I purchased a laundromat in southeast Washington, D.C., a stone's throw from the current Washington Nationals ballpark. As exciting as it was, being my first significant entrepreneurial venture, I was in over my head. The previous owner, an Indian gentleman named Ganesh, had employed two engineers who were also Indian, Shlok, and Dinesh. The engineers remained.

Up to this point in my life, I had not encountered many cultures other than middle-class African Americans and white Americans. Suddenly, an unexpected cultural difference involved personal space.

When I don't know someone well, whether personal or professional, it's natural for me to communicate standing four to six feet from the other person, generally the social norm in America. But because India is a collectivist society, personal space is not the norm. Indian families are very close physically and socially. A friend of mine who lives in India says it's common to have three generations under one roof. Given the social norms that I grew up with, I can only imagine the chaos this would cause.

Separation and distance were expected in my family. I grew up in a house with one sibling, and we had separate rooms and personal items. If one of us walked into the other's room without knocking, it meant war. My wife, Kerryann, is from Jamaica. She has nine siblings. She said no one had her own space when she was growing up. As a result, she had to share almost all of her personal items, including shoes, clothing, and hairbrushes. At times multiple relatives, new to Jamaica, would stay with her family for several months to a year. My experience is the polar opposite.

While speaking with Dinesh, the lead laundromat engineer, I remember feeling incredibly uncomfortable because he always stood so close. I would take two steps back, and Dinesh would take two steps forward. On one occasion, I began sweating because Dinesh was right in my face. Finally, I walked to the other side of a washing machine to continue the conversation. Although Dinesh never said anything, he looked at me like I had two heads.

Several weeks later, Dinesh resigned his position. Although Ashlock was still employed, he was entry level. Dinesh was the best engineer, and I had no experience fixing laundry equipment. I felt terrible that he left on account of my behavior. At the time, we were both oblivious to each other's cultural norms, so each time we engaged, we violated each other's boundaries. He was out the door, and I was up to my eyeballs in suds.

After Dinesh resigned, I asked Ashlock why. Outside of the social space issue, I thought Dinesh and I had a good relationship. Ashlock explained that Dinesh was under the impression that I didn't like him because I walked away during our conversations.

Because of my upbringing, it was not evident that putting space between us was a sign of disrespect. For the most part, my family didn't even eat dinner together. The only time I was physically close to others was when my friends came over and sat on the couch with me to play video games. Later on, I realized that this social norm was the cause of conflict for me and others with similar experiences. Most of us seem to move through life on autopilot, failing to consider the culture, perspectives, customs, and social norms of other people and what they feel is respectful and expect in return.

- What were some social norms in your family growing up?
- How did these social norms influence the way you see and interact with others?
- When you encounter a different social norm, does it make you feel uncomfortable or think that other people are wrong?

Although I tried to rehire Dinesh, he never came back. Shortly after, the laundromat failed. That experience will forever haunt me. Since then, I have learned to investigate others' norms before jumping to conclusions or taking personal offense. Although certain encounters still make me feel uncomfortable, somehow realizing that this makes it a little more comfortable.

Fast-forward to 2019. when I delivered a speech on inclusive leadership at the International Organizational Development Association conference in Viña del Mar, Chile. When I walked into the conference, the coordinator greeted me with a kiss on my cheek. Having spent most of my professional career in the States, her gesture made me feel uneasy. At that moment, I remembered my experience with Dinesh, so I returned the greeting. I quickly got over differences and awkward moments after meeting and making new friends with participants from India, Chile, Australia, France, and Canada.

3. What kind of music did you listen to growing up?

In any era or geographical location, you can tell what is happening based on the music the culture is producing. For example, during the civil rights movement in the United States, Marvin Gaye's "What's Going On" was popular. In the mid-1800s, during the Civil War, it was "Dixie." In the seventies, "Stayin' Alive" was the number one hit by the Bee Gees. The music we listen to timestamps the experiences and emotions we felt at that time. Do you remember what you were doing the first time you heard "Billie Jean" by Michael Jackson? Listening to a song can take us back to a time of joy, sadness, or even excitement. No matter what music you're listening to, it reflects culture.

Think about some of the music played in your house as you were growing up. Maybe you listened to the Rolling Stones "(I Can't Get No) Satisfaction," "Let's Twist Again" by Chubby Checker, or "Hey Jude" by the Beatles. Or maybe "Respect" by Aretha Franklin, "Mustang Sally" by Wilson Pickett, "Good Vibrations" by the Beach Boys, "Stand by Me" by Ben E. King, or "Fly Me to the Moon" by Frank Sinatra. These songs add to your zip code story. They help connect you to a time in your life that meant something to you. Nothing is like going to a concert or singing your favorite song in the car. It's even better when others know the song and sing along. Music builds connections and can even change our physiological state.

Did your family sing songs on long car rides when you were a kid, maybe even Christmas songs? Did you have songs that everyone in your school knew by heart? Was it Bon Jovi, Run-DMC, Aerosmith, Bruce Springsteen, Stevie Wonder, Queen, Whitney Houston, Elton John, or Billy Joel? I'm dropping these names because I want you to see how emotive music is and how it can take you to a different moment in life—perhaps a prior zip code, residence, relationship, or a different you. Understanding the music that was a part of our lives helps us understand our zip code story and those of others.

Music became a big part of my father's life because he didn't have television as a child. Oddly enough, music is also a big part of my daughters' lives, and they have a television—make that three. Still, they prefer to listen to music on their phones.

Black or white, music helps break barriers. Music is one area that crosses cultural and class boundaries. We often forget that African Americans and whites often have similar tastes in music, especially music created in one's generation. In terms of music, it doesn't matter if whites or blacks can identify with one another's culture, lifestyle, or even musical lyrics. What matters is they can find common ground and appreciate each other's creations, even when those creations are developed by people who experienced very different upbringings.

Many of us have heard and sung along to Eminem's number one hit, "Lose Yourself." The beat makes us move, and whether or not one grew up in a poor neighborhood like Eminem, many (even in the middle to upper class) can relate to struggle and hardship. Eminem's music transcends generations and cultures. He is one of many artists who have helped cultures assimilate. Living up to his last name and winning the hearts and minds of both blacks and whites, John Legend's "All of Me" speaks to the ideas of balance and compromise—something that all of us should try to exercise more often. Music brings people together, gives us the freedom to express our feelings, and helps bring our similarities to light.

4. Which era did you grow in, and what were some of the most significant artifacts of your time?

As a diversity and inclusion consultant, one of the biggest challenges I encounter in companies outside of race and gender differences is generational differences. Understanding the era from which one came can be influential. When I stand in front of a room of three different generations—millennials, Generation X, and baby boomers—I can get each group to shake their heads, clap, and comment simply by speaking about relatable topics. Gen Xers will perk up their ears when they hear me say that I was a "latchkey kid." When I talk about working hard, being punctual, firm handshakes, and food rations, baby boomers will relate. When I want to get the attention of millennials and Gen Zs, I talk about technology, apps, electric cars, and cryptocurrency.

Each generation has an idea of the epochs before and after their time, but their experiences in the era they grew up in hold more meaning. Whether in the workplace or our personal lives, the generation from which we were born, raised, and matured into adulthood shapes our perspectives more than many of us know or can understand.

If you plan to be successful in business, it's essential to learn about the culture, gender, generational backgrounds, and languages of others. "By 2030, nearly 83 million people will have entered the workforce, with more than two-thirds projected to replace retiring workers. The population that will replace aging Baby Boomers will be a combination of Hispanics, Blacks, Asians, Pacific Islanders, and Native Americans."[3]

5. Did you or your family members have hobbies when you were growing up?

Family hobbies are meaningful activities that shape the way we engage with others. If you grew up in a household where Sunday night football was a big deal, you may continue the tradition or go in the opposite direction. Many of my white friends spent their childhood taking family trips to swim at a nearby lake or beach.

Friends and colleagues have told me they learned to swim on these family outings. Unfortunately, many of my African American friends did not have this experience. Their version of swimming usually looks more like them trying to save their lives. They're not comfortable in a setting where they have to exercise their swimming skills—activities such as swimming draw a line between social classes. Those who are more affluent can engage in golf and equestrianism because they can afford it and had lessons or exposure in their youth.

Activities or things of mutual interest are the biggest challenges for building relationships across class and culture. However, when you have nothing else to connect to or talk about with someone, you can always lean on sports or similar activities such as traveling or education.

When two people find it hard to connect to one another's hobbies and leisure activities, the relationship can feel strained. Class migrants often have little, other than work, to create a shared reality around, so it becomes a barrier to build relationships with those from a higher social class.

It's best not to underestimate people. Some class migrants have had experiences that many in the professional world have as well. Many local government agencies and nonprofit organizations strive to make more hobbies and extracurricular activities available for low-income and marginalized families. In the business world, it's helpful to keep others' backgrounds in mind and keep the conversation going; eventually, we learn that we have more in common than we think. Most of us can connect by speaking about our children, local restaurants, movies, television series, books we have read, and if all else fails, use light humor. The best advice is to let down your guard and be genuine.

Speaking about my education, travels, and outings to the symphony help me connect, build relationships, and increase trust with those with whom I engage today. Others may talk about sports; that's always a safe bet—unless you root for an unfavorable team. In other words, if you're a Mets fan and you live in Philadelphia, you may want to keep that to yourself until you get to know that person.

A big part of social class is answering the question, "Do I fit in here?" When you have had similar experiences and can talk about those experiences in detail, those who have had the same experiences develop trust and kinship. Building trusting relationships can lead to career opportunities, business opportunities, invitations to personal functions such as dinner parties, which can help you expand your network and influence.

Hobbies and experiences can feel foreign to us if we haven't had the exposure, so we tend to label them cultural taboos. I can't tell you how many times I've heard a person of color say black people don't do that. One time I posted a weekend ski trip on social media. Shortly after, I got a call from one of my longtime African American friends. He said something like, "Hey, I saw your Facebook post. I notice you're doing white people stuff. What's up with that?" Another friend phoned me after I posted a horseback riding trip and said, "I see you like doing white people stuff. That is cool! But be careful; I don't know if people of color are supposed to be riding on horses." I didn't get mad because I knew we had two different zip code stories.

I was and still am expanding my zip code story in a way that makes my friends uncomfortable. Class migrants face a double bind. At times, they can feel as if they don't fit into either story. Class migrants need to find a balance. Often, organizations hold skiing trips or other trips to resorts at a discount; this is a good way for class migrants to gain new experiences until they earn disposable income. If you're a class migrant, take advantage of workplace invitations to outings, lunch jogs, barbecues, parties, and so on. These are opportunities to develop memories, things to laugh about, and things that create a shared reality.

6. What did your parents do for a living, and how has that shaped your choices?

In my early twenties, I interviewed business owners quite a bit. Bob Baker, a gentleman who owned an insurance company, became my mentor. He said people learn about wealth around the dinner table, not in school. In addition, when I would meet colleagues and friends who had extensive vocabularies, they said most of what they learned came from their parents. They would say it is just the way we talk in our house. Some of my friends who use foul language also admitted that their parents used the same language. So not only do we learn about investing and vocabulary from our parents, but we also are exposed to career opportunities through their career choices and networks of influence.

My dad was an electrician. When I was older, he took me along to different jobs. All of his friends were blue-collar workers. Many of them used curse words in their everyday speech, not because they were angry but because it was just part of their vocabulary. My dad would often go out and have drinks with them. My mom was a semiprofessional government worker. Although she worked in an office, her position did not require a degree. She was able to travel quite often and work with engineers who had college degrees. My parents' occupations initially shaped my visions of what I should be and what was possible in terms of a job or career.

Whether it be a blue-collar job or a white-collar career, our parents' occupations influence our possibilities and aspirations. In addition, our family members, teachers, coaches, and neighbors all impact our career choices.

As you consider your zip code story, go back as far as possible and think about what you wanted to be when you were a kid. I am not talking about when you were six and wanted to be an astronaut; I'm talking about when you became serious about your career. Where were you first exposed to the opportunity? Where did you find encouragement to follow this path, or did you fall into your career?

7.   Did your family engage in religious or spiritual practice?

The business world has two golden rules; never bring religion or politics into the workplace. But, of course, if you work for a religious institution, that's different. Our faith, or lack of it, shapes our moral compass. It can subconsciously and consciously dictate what we believe to be right or wrong for ourselves and others. Some people attended churches or synagogues when they were children. Some went to temple and prayed five times a day, and others were not exposed to any spiritual or religious practices while growing up. Religious and spiritual practices are deeply held beliefs about faith, life, and death.

When others do not hold the same beliefs or believe in something completely different, it can cause conflict and create silos. The point is, we should all consider how our religious and spiritual practices or the lack of them shape the way we show up and the way we see others in our personal and professional lives.

8.   Did you experience crime in your home or neighborhood?

Before writing this book, I never considered how exposure to crime as a child shapes our interactions with others. To this day, I can only reflect on the impact that crime has on its victims. In my twenties, I attended the Maryland Drafting Institute, a technology and engineering school located in Langley Park, Maryland. At the time, I took the tradesman route because I thought I wanted to be an engineer. James, a classmate, and I would drive to school every morning and talk about our life experiences. He had grown up in Washington, D.C., a much different experience than I had growing up in the suburbs. James constantly joked about me living on a farm because he thought I lived so far from the city. After a few weeks, I noticed that anytime we talked about money, like paying for gas if I was driving, he became very defensive. Later on, we talked about how his experience with neighborhood crime made him more paranoid and sometimes aggressive toward those he thought were trying to manipulate him or steal from him. Although we were friends, he constantly questioned my motives. I found this to be the case with other people I've met who had experiences with neighborhood crime. Many of them were apprehensive about trusting others with things of value such as money and personal items.

In contrast, I developed friendships with people who came from Iran and Russia and other war-struck countries. They did not exhibit a lack of trust; they just seemed more assertive and direct. They also did not seem to value material things like my friends who lived in inner cities. Instead, these individuals valued spending time with family and building meaningful relationships. If you're a manager, it's essential to understand the class migrant experience, especially if others came from an inner city or a developing country where crime may be more prevalent.

Here are some additional questions to help you better understand your zip code story:

- What books did you grow up reading?
- What type of schools did you attend? For example, was it a Catholic school, all-girl or all-boy school, Montessori school, study abroad, special needs, charter, or emerging school?
- Did you grow up in a two-parent or single-parent household?
- What was the highest level of education your parents and other adults achieved when you were a child?
- Where did your family go on vacation when you were a child?
- Were your parents working class, professionals, or business owners?
- Did you play sports as a child?
- Were you the oldest child?
- Was it OK in your family to make mistakes?
- Did you feel your family was financially secure?
- Which television shows did you grow up watching?
- Did your family have a pet?
- Did you have a family member or a friend with a mental, emotional, physical, visual, hearing, or learning disability?
- Did you experience diversity in your family, in your neighborhood, or in social activities growing up?

As a reminder, for each question ask yourself these follow-up questions: How does your answer affect how you see the world now? How did the answer make you feel as a child?

Your background is multilayered. Some of those layers involve culture, including social norms, educational experiences, religious experiences, political affiliations, experiences traveling to different countries, playing sports, parental guidance, and so on. Some of our backgrounds come from vicarious experiences. For some of us, the books we've read and the stories we've heard at home, through media and print, shape the way we see the world.

Years ago, I worked with a group of leaders who traveled to the States from Haiti. We had just finished a training seminar, and I decided to show them Washington, D.C. I thought they might want to see the Air and Space Museum because it's a big attraction among the Smithsonian museums. It's also my favorite. As we walked through the Washington, D.C., mall, the whole group from Haiti came to a complete stop. I didn't realize they had stopped until I was on the other side of the street. I was frustrated because I wanted to get to the Air and Space Museum before it closed.

When I walked back across the street, all twelve people in the group were staring at an ice-skating rink. I could not understand what was so fascinating. I asked, "What are you looking at? Haven't you ever seen snow and ice?" One man looked at me with a straight face and said, "No, we have not; we only read about it." It had not dawned on me that their experiences were so different than mine. They had only read about ice-skating rinks, which made sense because they live in a tropical climate. Their zip code story in this regard was the polar opposite of mine. In addition, I learned that they weren't too interested in the Air and Space Museum, not like I was anyway.

People differ on many levels. One exercise that I engage my clients in is called "I am, but I am not." People share an identity that they associate with and a stereotype that's untrue about their identity. Most people enjoy playing along. And they are usually passionate about a stereotype about their identity that's false. This passion typically stems from an experience that has held them back or made them feel left out or demeaned. But the reality is, it's a part of their zip code story.

Few understand how their zip code can shape their choices, opportunities, and possibilities. Before we close this chapter, I want to share one man's journey to illustrate the value of education, access, and self-development and how embracing each changed his life story for the better.

Chris Wilson played chess and cello as a boy. He can speak Spanish, Italian, and Mandarin and is now the founder and owner of the

House of DaVinci and Barclay Investment Corporation. Based on his achievements, you might think that Chris was from a Beverly Hills zip code, but Chris was born and raised in the underbelly of Washington, D.C. Notably, he never let it define him or his story.

Chris grew up in a crime and poverty-stricken neighborhood afflicted with drugs, gunfire, and police brutality. He faced abuse and violence in his home, school, and community. By day, Chris walked in fear. By night, he slept on the floor to avoid stray bullets. As a child, his brother was shot, and he had lost five friends to gun violence.

After bearing witness to the kidnapping, shooting, and burial of a close family member, Chris feared for his life and took another person's life in defense.

Subsequently, at the age of 17, Chris was incarcerated for murder. After serving over 16 years, a judge released Chris from prison contingent on him completing a self-improvement plan that he was developing in prison.

Chris called it his master plan, a strategic plan where he would earn a degree and teach himself to read, write, and speak in several foreign languages. Chris achieved those things and then launched a high-end furniture company and a construction contracting company. He then authored his first book, *The Master Plan*, published in 2019, landing him an interview with Trevor Noah on *The Daily Show*, an Emmy- and Peabody Award–winning program.

Chris's experiences, introspections, and journey from the streets of crime to entrepreneurial success have taught him a lot about life. He shares some simple truths about growth, class, and the similarities that unite people.

Oftentimes, as people, we all honestly, regardless of class, we all want the same things in life, right. We want a house, a roof over our head, to do impactful work and spend time with our families. So, at the end of the day, it is those things that I understand that regardless of class, we all have those things in common, and so I try to find things to discuss that we all care about, and doing that allows you to bond with people. Once people like you, they do not have a problem doing business with you, making a phone call, sending an email on your behalf, or sharing information.

Class is also about access to information. I have realized that people in the upper class are avid readers. They read everything; they read the newspapers and every book. The majority of my friends in that particular class share books. They might say read this book, check out this magazine, did you see this article, and what do you think the implications are? Anybody can do it. . . So I think reading and embracing education, whatever you can get going online—YouTube videos and articles [*sic*] is something anybody can do. But folks in the upper class make it a priority to do it. Everyone has the opportunity to hack that information by going to the library, reading books, and reaching out to people who are not like them. (Chris Wilson, interview by author, "Simple truths about growth, class, and the similarities that unite people," n.d.)

Education, access, self-development, and a solid plan gave Chris a second chance. It allowed him to change his story and overcome unimaginable social and personal barriers, beliefs, and biases. Because of Chris's mental fortitude, he emerged from a hostile home culture, violent zip code, and life in prison to became a successful business person and social justice advocate. In chapter 5, I'll share some steps to help you develop a master plan.

4

Zip Code Bias

It's not at all hard to understand a person; it's only hard to listen
without bias.[1] —Criss Jami, American poet, author of *Healology*[1]

Few people like to hear that they are biased or think of themselves
as biased, but bias is something to which everyone is subject. When
we hear the term bias, it strikes a discordant note because it makes
us feel immoral or unfair. However, biases are not biased; it's something each of us has in common. And it helps to understand that
bias is malleable. That means we can learn to become aware of our
biases and form new associations. We are not stuck with our biases
for eternity.

Research shows that implicit bias is a "behavioral phenomenon
rather than a mental structure ... (it) is something that people
do rather than something that people possess. More specifically,
implicit bias can be defined as implicit group-based behavior, which
is behavior that is influenced in an implicit manner by cues that
function as an indicator of the social group to which others belong."[2]

The behavioral perspective lets us lower our defenses and curb
our self-loathing toward bias. We can now recognize that because
bias is a behavioral rather than a mental construct, a "behavioral
perspective does not assign blame for biased behavior but simply implies that the behavior is a function of social cues in the

environment."[3] Biases influence reasoning, judgment, and the decisions we make for ourselves and others.

As the chapter and my story unfold, we will explore a few universal biases that demonstrate how they can propel or limit our actions and how they emanate from simple heuristics. Also called a rule of thumb, cognitive heuristics are shortcuts that we use based on our knowledge, experiences, and level of thinking. We rely on heuristics and engage system-1[4] thinking or fast thinking[5] to save time and expedite our next course of action. Before we go any further, let's define bias: "a prejudice, leaning, inclination, bent, predilection, proneness, propensity, proclivity, tendency, feeling; fixed idea, preconceived idea, preconception, narrow view, slant, one-sidedness, unfairness" . . . and so on.[6] No wonder it causes tension and hot debates!

Again, bias is not exclusive of how we view people who differ from us. Bias shapes our rationale, our choices, and our self-view. Although implicit bias is a behavioral perspective, some biases are innate, such as those that help us avoid danger. In general, biases are learned from observations, experiences, socialization, and long-held beliefs that have been instilled by our upbringing, community, and the media we chose to listen to—because of our predispositions.

Bias does not discriminate. Bias is not something you contract or develop because you're a bad person. More often than not, we are not conscious of our biases. You could hold a PhD or be a high-school dropout. You could grow up in the Sun Belt in the United States or Kensington Palace Gardens in London. You could come from royalty or poverty. Whichever way you spin it, each of us has established biases that we are not fully aware of or understand. Our biases develop over time, and they are learned and reinforced by in-group social cues and our primary culture and the subcultures to which we have or have not been exposed in our lives thus far.

Before we dive into other forms of bias, I want to share Megha Don Bosco's story so you can see how biases influence our decisions.

Megha Don Bosco is the co-founder and partner of an organizational development consulting firm. Megha is a second-generation class migrant born and raised in India; one of her parents came from old money, and the other identifies as a class migrant. Although Megha did not have the financial hardships that most class migrants face, she experienced gender bias. Here's a look at her perspective on privilege, social class influences, and gender bias.

If I was born a son, I would have to be very well educated. Everyone would be like, "You need to study more, get your Ph.D." That is important. For me, when I was 21 years old, I was told to think "just complete your education." My parents were already talking about marriage. . . . In my state, in Kerala itself, if I [sic] compare a Christian family versus a Hindu family, there is always a lot of importance given to education, even for a girl. She needs to complete her education before she even thinks about getting married. In my case, on the other hand, it was "you can always study after marriage." Who is stopping you from studying after marriage? It is almost like as long as you have a good enough resume to get married, that is good enough. It is not so much about building your career or thinking about what this individual wants to help this person grow and feel confident. But it is almost like, get married to a rich husband. A lot to do with it is mindset. Mindset comes from upbringing, and that upbringing when it has certain privileges, it is easy to say that you need to have that kind of mindset.

On the other hand, coming from an upper-class family has its advantages. For example, I remember when I was little, I would always say, "Money comes, money goes. If money goes, there are ways to make more money.'" But it is very easy to say that from the standpoint of privilege.

I cannot give advice to someone who is coming from a different class. It is unfair because you need to have this kind of luxury to even think that way. You want that knowledge and comfort more than anything else. There is so much comfort in every situation. It is not just physical comfort. There is also psychological comfort, mental comfort, and emotional comfort. There are so many things to knowing that there is [sic] monetary backup; it influences your decisions, who you pick as your mate and your career choices.

I mean, at the end of the day, class and wealth have a lot of advantages. It helped my parents and grandparents set me up for where I am today. . . . I am already thinking about securing my next generation. I want [sic] my daughter to be independent, successful, have a wonderful career, and all of that. . . . Still, tomorrow, if my daughter wants to do something that is not going to generate more revenue, but it is her passion, this allows her to do that.(Megha Don Bosco, interview by author, "How biases can influence our decisions," n.d.)

Bias has to be taught. If you hear your parents downgrading women or people of different backgrounds, why, you are going to do that. —Barbara Bush

Bias leads us to things that bring pleasure and lead us away from things that make us feel uncomfortable or bring pain. When we first form an impression of someone, we make judgments based on what we know. When someone or something is unfamiliar, we typically anchor onto a collection of preexisting data or similar characteristics of someone or something to try to make sense of it. Absent reflection, gathering facts, and system-2 thinking, we take mental shortcuts that often lack the data required to make sound judgments. The result is faulty assumptions. These assumptions (true or not) are called confirmation biases,[7] and they act like self-fulfilling prophecies. Because we expect a specific outcome or anticipate certain behaviors from a particular person, we tend to zero in on signs that confirm that our assumptions are correct while ignoring information that counters our assumptions.

FEARS AND BIAS ARE CONDITIONED

Some researchers claim that humans are born with only two fears: fear of falling and fear of loud noises. Based on this, all other fears are learned or conditioned from experiences and social cues within our particular culture. "Fear can be learned through direct experience with a threat, but it can also be learned via social means such as verbal warnings or observing others."[8]

Think about that. What's one of the first words a child learns to say? You may include mommy, daddy, and no. Most parents are excited when they hear their child speak their parental title for the first time. Most are not enthusiastic about hearing the word "no" come out of their child's mouth. But who taught the child this word? The parent taught the child to say "no" reflexively, without thinking. By telling the child "no" repeatedly, the child adopts the word not fully knowing what it means—but more than aware of its implications.

Later in life, the child will learn the impact of "no" and how to use it more effectively. The child also learns other words and gestures such as smiling, hugging, and asking for what he wants, repeatedly, until he gets it. These are all forms of conditioning or learned behaviors. For the child to survive, he must learn quickly to ask for what he wants, such as food or attention, and learn what not to do through pain or discomfort.

We're all kind of like big babies, aren't we? We've unconsciously learned to navigate our environment by understanding what causes us pain and what causes us pleasure. The brain helps us do this through bias. As we experience new things, the brain uses preferences, perception, and interpretation to bring certain pieces of data in our environment to our attention. The other data fades to the background, which some refer to as blind spots. When the brain perceives certain information as irrelevant, it will fail to bring it to your attention or awareness. The brain does this to make sure your conscious mind does not become overwhelmed with information. We call this information overload, especially in the twenty-first century. When this happens, our brain is overwhelmed with information and cannot process it, which leads to mental fatigue and frustration, both of which prevent us from taking action. From a primitive or primal perspective, the brain uses this data to protect us from harm or pain. It also uses the data to let us know our environment is safe.

If you're driving down the highway and a car ahead suddenly slams on its brakes, you most likely will hit the brakes, too. Without even thinking, we automatically jump into action to protect ourselves. That's learned behavioral bias, and it provokes awareness.

The brake bias happens in a matter of milliseconds. The brain taps your past experience for information that identifies the danger and triggers immediate action. You may also experience sweaty palms and increased heart rate. Without active cognition, your brain inputs data that determines a threat and moves your body into immediate action. This is the benefit of bias and how it protects us.

Some people see bias as a negative. On the contrary, bias is neither positive nor negative. A colleague of mine once described it this way: "Bias is a function of the brain that allows you to make decisions very quickly."[9] On the other hand, in a situation where we don't have enough information to determine whether or not it's safe, we may intuitively declare the situation unsafe. It's the default. When we experience such situations without awareness, intention, or control in our personal and professional lives, the default can hold us back from new opportunities and exclude others. I've identified a couple of experiences from my own zip code story to help illustrate this point.

Chapter 4

THE MOVE TO REISTERSTOWN

For almost thirty-nine years, I lived in Prince George's County, Maryland, a predominantly African American community. During this time, I had traveled little and internationally, not at all. Because I wanted my daughter Christen to be in a multicultural school, I moved to Reisterstown, Maryland, despite my fears. The move terrified me because all of my experiences had been in Prince George's County among similar people.

I had never left Prince George's County for an extended time. The only travel memories from my childhood were visiting my godsister, who lived near Virginia Beach, and my mother's family in Florida. I'll admit, I was always curious and dreamed of exploring new places, but my fears always shut down those dreams.

Still, I made a hesitant decision to move to Reisterstown, but only after dating the same woman for more than three years and realizing the importance of my daughter attending a multicultural school. I felt intimidated by the new environment, concerned about the prospects of developing new relationships for my daughter and me, especially with most of our friends and family rooted in Prince George's County.

But we moved. I knew no one. Everything and everyone was foreign. People didn't necessarily look or dress differently from what I was accustomed to; I was in a different environment with different social norms and protocols. I lived close to Main Street, which was the main thoroughfare through the small town. Reisterstown is a small, older community founded in 1758 by John Reister, a German immigrant. Although Reisterstown was a diverse, family-oriented community with untold social and educational benefits for my girls, it was not Prince George's County. Not one store, street, or person was recognizable.

Reisterstown was only an hour ride from our former home, but moving there made a world of difference in my zip code story. Meeting people who grew up outside Prince George's County opened my eyes to different cultures, traditions, and social norms. It made me reevaluate my fears, beliefs, and biases about people and life in general.

The area offered different cultural activities and the opportunity to build friendships with people from different backgrounds. During this time, I attended a family-friendly pig race and tried trap shooting, a sport where you use a shotgun to shoot launched saucer-shaped clay targets.

More than anything, the move changed my perspectives, debunked my biases, and changed my viewpoints about life and me. I realized that some people spoke, dressed, and did things differently than me but held similar values and dreamed of the same things in life. It took about a year, but I adjusted to my new surroundings and made new friends, as did my two daughters.

I also realized that I could move anywhere and thrive. No doubt, I struggled at first, living in a new and strange area, but my daughters and I benefited immensely from the opportunity. My oldest daughter, Christen, finally found her tribe at Franklin High School, which both daughters attended and graduated. Christen joined the performing arts department and quickly made the area home.

She flourished in the academic and social diversity the school and the area had to offer. A year and a half later, my youngest daughter, Lauren, who had previously lived with her mother in Prince George's County, joined us in Reisterstown. Not only did she make new friends, but she also picked up two new languages, Spanish and Korean. She learned Spanish in class and Korean from her new friends.

This move was monumental in terms of personal growth and development for all three of us. It introduced us to new possibilities and changed the course of our lives. My biases and fears about moving almost got the best of me. I know now that my mind reflexively evoked biases to keep me safe, to keep the status quo, but had I not swallowed my fears and taken the chance to relocate, it would have held back my family and me from becoming who we are today.

Sometimes our biases keep us from moving forward and reaching our full potential.

GOING INTERNATIONAL

Eighteen years ago, when I first began speaking to audiences in the local community centers and churches, I would have never thought that I'd be speaking to people in different countries who spoke different languages. In my first speech, I was beyond nervous—I was scared stiff. Today, I love getting up in front of people and sharing my thoughts. The personal development I underwent in

Reisterstown inspired me to reach for my dreams. That extended reach brought my dreams of becoming a motivational speaker to reality. My transformation did not happen overnight, certainly not without its challenges, humiliations, and setbacks.

If there is no struggle, there is no progress. —Frederick Douglass

My first speaking engagement was horrible. I was asked to speak to a large group of children at the Glassmanor Community Center in Oxon Hill, Maryland. From the day I accepted the request, I felt a knot in my stomach. I had a few mini panic attacks. I couldn't sleep for a week. I went over my speech twenty times, but it didn't seem to help. I walked into the community center sweating bullets and thinking up a million what-ifs and worst-case scenarios.

Then the funniest thing happened right before my presentation. To calm my nerves, I went to the community center gym to lift free weights. I walked over to the bench press, lay down, and proceeded to chest press a relatively light weight. Suddenly, the bar started leaning to the left. Before I knew it, all the weights thundered to the floor. Everyone in the gym stopped to look at me. In my haste and anxiety, I had forgotten to add another twenty-five-pound weight plate to the right side of the bar, so the weight distribution was lopsided. Even worse, my imminent audience, the kids attending my workshop, coincidentally walked by as the weights crashed. I heard one them say, "I hope that guy isn't going to be our speaker tonight."

A few minutes later, as I walked into the gymnasium where my workshop was held, I could hear a few kids snickering. When I started speaking, it seemed like all my thoughts were coming out jumbled. Thankfully, this was before every kid had a smartphone, so they just started looking around and talking to one another. I felt like a bumbling idiot. But lucky for me, Kenneth, my speaking mentor, was there. When Kenneth saw that I was crashing worse than the weight plates, he quickly jumped in and started to engage the kids with humor and relevant questions. Thanks to Kenneth, the workshop turned out well.

After that catastrophic speaking engagement, I was even more insecure about my role. I started to develop a negative bias against speaking in front of people because I allowed the kids' disinterest to confirm my worst fears—that people would not pay attention while

I was speaking. If not for Kenneth pushing me to get more experience, I likely would have continued to believe that I was a failure and not cut out for public speaking—this is the confirmation bias I mentioned earlier.

> We gain strength, and courage, and confidence by each experience in which we really stop to look fear in the face . . . we must do that which we think we cannot. —Eleanor Roosevelt

We tend to latch onto preconceived ideas and negative thoughts and beliefs because of our experiences or what we think we know at that moment. Kenneth helped me see the debacle for what it was—a growth opportunity. He made me realize that I could not possibly predict my future based on one bad experience and essentially put me on a path to becoming an international motivational speaker.

Too often, I have allowed my negative self-talk and biases for other people to get in the way of progress. When I first started speaking to diverse audiences, I was uncomfortable. For example, I thought whites would never relate to my stories because my background was limited, and my contacts, engagements, and interactions mainly had been with other Blacks. In my zip code, I simply did not have a lot of exposure to different cultures. So, naturally, I had developed a bias against other cultures. It took plenty of time and effort to work through this bias because it was deep rooted. Yet today, my engagements and audience are diverse.

These experiences have helped me become a better speaker, but I could easily have allowed my biases to prevent me from advancing.

IMPOSTOR SYNDROME

Howard J. Ross, founder of the diversity consulting firm Cook Ross, frequently talks about his experiences with impostor syndrome. Howard has been a social justice advocate for more than thirty years and speaks internationally, yet he says he still contends with impostor syndrome. Many famous people have expressed the same sentiment. Nevertheless, I believe one reason people succeed is that they continue to do things they have never done before. Not surprisingly, then, successful people tend to suffer from impostor syndrome more often than others.

Let me explain.

When you do the same thing every day for twenty years, you're unlikely to feel like an impostor. Your brain says, "We've done this before. We have tons of experience. We definitely know what we're talking about." But when you try something new, you're in uncharted territory. Your brain surges into overdrive because it does not have enough information to tell whether it's safe to move forward. And many people never move forward. They allow their twenty-years-and-counting zip code biases to get in the way. Instead of saying to themselves, "You know I'm just afraid because I've never done this before. I'll find someone to help me or read some books or come up with a plan," they say, "Oh, that's not for people like me"; or "I don't have enough education"; or "People where I come from don't do things like that."

Unfortunately, those self-deniers typically do not hang with people who will push them out of their comfort zone. They usually hang with familiar faces—people just like them or people who make them feel at ease with their zip code story. When we hang out with people who make us feel comfortable or have a similar zip code story, we don't grow. You can't expand your zip code story when all your friends and colleagues have the same story.

Class migrants can feel like impostors in the business world. It's not because they lack educational credentials or because they are a racial minority in a company. It's because they are speaking, dressing, and interacting in a way that is the opposite of their zip code. In other words, they can feel as though they are living two separate lives. Feeling as if they are underappreciated or not taken seriously, they walk on eggshells at work and at home. The zip code stories conflict and counter each other. If they still reside in their original zip code but work in an uptown business district, they can feel like an impostor to their family and friends. Some report dissonance between their zip code roles and perceive dismissive treatment from the community for flouting social norms within the neighborhood zip code.

Initially, when I told my friends that I was going to be a motivational speaker, some of them laughed; others gave me a sympathetic, "Sounds good." In their defense, I was a serial entrepreneur who frequently came up with different ideas. So, based on what they had known about me in the past, they couldn't take me seriously. To them, I was merely chasing another pipe dream.

Although hindsight is 20/20, if I had never moved outside my zip code or evolved into a new zip code story, I doubt I would have received the support I needed to overcome my biases. To overcome my zip code bias, I sought mentors, joined Toastmasters International, visited the local chapter of the National Speakers Association, listened to audio programs, and spoke for free as often as I could. I had to believe in myself when few others would.

Everyone has a zip code bias because everyone comes from a zip code, and everyone develops biases. Looking at our biases in relation to our zip code can help us understand them better. If you realize that all your friends have similar zip code stories, it's easier to see how you might have a bias in that area. But if someone said, "Hey, I think you're biased because you don't have friends of different ethnicities," you might take offense. Understanding your zip code story lets you reverse engineer where you might have bias. For example, if you love country music because you grew up listening to it, you may not favor or tolerate classical or hip-hop. Understanding your zip code story helps you connect the dots and become more open and understanding of different people and their experiences.

THE THIRTY-FIVE-YEAR-OLD SWIMMER

We are a product of our culture, which extends beyond the environment. I mentioned earlier in this book that culture encompasses the accepted social norms within your environment. When I was a kid, we went to the pool to swim even though most of us didn't know how to swim. We would splash around in the shallow end or close to the sides—to keep from drowning. That's what I thought swimming was: splashing around to keep from drowning. As a father, I took my daughters to the pool. And guess what? I taught them to swim the best way I knew how: splash around and keep from drowning. That's all I knew.

In my mid-thirties, I started going to the community pool in my subdivision, where I noticed both kids and adults were actually swimming—freestyle, breaststroke, backstroke—up and down the lanes. They were not splashing around. I thought to myself, I want to be able to swim like that—and without fear that I will drown. But I had a slight problem; I didn't know how to swim.

I could have taken a class, but I was embarrassed because I felt too old to learn to swim. So, instead of taking classes, I started asking people how they do it. One person answered, "Do what?" "Swim the length of the pool without drowning," I said. "I don't know," he said. "I just do it because I learned when I was a kid."

A different zip code. A different story. But I recognized the limitation of my own swimming zip code story even as my fear kicked in about drowning. It's a story I share with many other African Americans. Blacks don't swim. Now, of course, many do, but this is a perceived norm for many African Americans.

It's not too shocking to learn that my parents couldn't swim either. A 2017 YMCA study disclosed that swimming ability for African Americans is heavily influenced by parental swimming ability and encouragement. So, I had a good reason not to be a swimmer! The study also found that water-safety knowledge and fear of drowning were two other factors that influenced whether a child would swim.[10] Both factors applied to me. Other myths circulating within Black communities have been captured in a short documentary, *Blacks Can't Swim*. The film flouts arguably racist reasons such as "Your bones are too dense," or "Blacks can't even float." "It's just not a priority within the minority community."[11] All of this leads us back to the idea of cultural capital and the beliefs that we inherit from our families.

Biases and fears are not only conditioned; they are also responsible for stereotypes and keeping those biases and stereotypes going. They limit both the stereotyper and the stereotypee. Since the dawn of time, cultures have learned and evolved from one another. When we automatically believe that a whole race doesn't enjoy, participate, or wish to participate in any activities that other cultures enjoy and join in, we automatically confirm those biases by excluding them. Just as white people like Cajun shrimp, hip-hop, and basketball, Black people like to swim, skydive, snowboard, and shoot skeet.

Look no further for swim examples than Maritza Correia, who took the gold in the 2002 National Championship; or Cullen Jones, Simone Manuel, or Lia Neal, all Olympic-level swimmers. As for skydiving, Will Smith took the plunge, as did African American military veterans Nicholas Walker, Danielle Williams, and many others who have been skydiving for years. Russell Winfield may be the first Black pro snowboarder, but Blacks have been sliding down mountain slopes for decades. In terms of skeet shooting, Obama may have been the first Black president, but he's not the only Black person to shoot skeet at Camp David or otherwise.

Although it's true that a large percentage of Black children cannot swim, and some don't have access or resources, others adopt a bias story as an excuse for not getting out of their comfort zone—something the entire human race is guilty of at one time or another.

So, how did I exit my comfort zone and break away from my swimming bias? After meditating one day, an idea came to me: I want to swim. Then, this thought mushroomed into a strong desire: I must swim—up and down the lane.

I had finally decided that I was not only going to swim, but I was going to swim laps—no matter what. That very day I bought some goggles at Walmart. I drove to the pool, jumped in—at the side—and submerged myself to watch people swim. I observed their form, how they moved their arms and legs, and how many breaths they took before putting their face back in the water.

When a lane was free, I tried to freestyle the entire pool's length. The first thing I noticed was my form; it was all wrong. I was trying to swim to save my life, not to make it across the pool. Once I changed my form and practiced side breathing, I made it from one side of the pool to the other. And I wasn't fearful of drowning because I was too focused on what I was trying to accomplish.

CLASS MIGRANTS GETTING THEIR FEET WET

Class migrants and managers of class migrants must consider culture, inherited biases, and fears in a business setting. Literally, they are not underwater, but still, class migrants need to get the lay of the land, observe the inner workings of the office environment, rules, form, and social norms. Class migrants often swim against the current to get an education, which reflects their strong drive to succeed, and many start off in overdrive like I did when splashing to save my life. However, in a work setting, class migrants require more than goggles, observations, and desire. They know not to splash around and draw attention to their needs, but they need guidance on what "stroke" to practice, where and how to practice. They didn't grow up with parents who could show them how to swim (i.e., prepare them for business and give them practice honing business protocols). Most class migrants did not have the opportunity to participate in marketing programs and associations that build leadership skills, provide business-related role-playing scenarios, and hold problem-solving events such as DECA (Distributive Education Clubs of America).

Without being introduced to the business world at a young age, many class migrants find it hard to swim, much less advance. They struggle to keep their heads above water. Therefore, mentors or managers need to be aware of their own biases and culture and the biases, fears, struggles, and culture that class migrants inherit.

With time and the help of mentors, my pool performance improved. I swam into deep water and increased the number of laps I could do before exhaustion. The progress I made incentivized me to join the YMCA. The opportunity to swim year-round and make friends with advanced swimmers helped me refine stroke techniques and develop new skills and abilities. I made a big splash! I succeeded at swimming because I sought instruction, learned new techniques, and practiced amply. The change in the environment itself benefited me immensely. I went from hanging around people who just splashed when warm outside to hobnobbing with competitive swimmers. It wasn't without challenges.

The first day in the pool, I expected to drown. The pool was longer than most of the pools I had swum in before. Somehow, I managed to swim three laps but felt like I was going under at any point. Then something happened that helped me turn a new leaf. A woman in the lane next to me took a break and turned to address me. She said she wasn't "feeling herself," so she had only completed seventeen laps. Breathing heavily from exertion, I felt embarrassed because I had barely completed three laps, so I nodded to acknowledge her. She continued to talk; then I realized she hadn't said seventeen laps; she had said seventy! Then and there, I decided to find a way to improve, so I began thinking about two major obstacles: getting enough oxygen and lack of technique. That's when I noticed some people swam with a face mask and snorkel, which allowed them to see and breathe while they swam.

This was a game-changer. Off to Amazon I went in search of a face mask. With this gear, over the course of one day, I went from swimming three laps to twenty. Then in a few short months, fifty laps. Today, I swim an average of forty laps.

Swimming laps increased my self-confidence. Because I was more confident swimming in the pool, I felt confident swimming in the ocean—minus the fear of sharks—thanks to Shark Week, which the

Discovery Channel and the news media tend to hype all summer. While visiting Hawaii, I signed up for a free scuba diving lesson. Before the instructors take you into the ocean, they make sure you are comfortable swimming in a pool with all the gear. So that's where we started. Five resort guests and I slipped on wetsuits and flippers and strapped air tanks to our backs.

I thought it would be just like swimming in the pool. I thought wrong. I had to take each breath through my mouth because the goggles did not cover my whole face like those I wear to swim laps in the pool.

Once submerged in the pool, I watched people freak out. We were all uncomfortable, continually bobbing to the surface. It was clear most of us were not used to swimming with scuba gear and having to breathe through our mouths. After a one-hour scuba lesson, the instructor asked too keenly, "Okay, who's ready to go in the ocean?" No one raised their hand except for me.

> Do not let what you cannot do interfere with what you can do.
> —John Wooden

I had come this far, and I wasn't turning back. I confronted my biases and fears and washed them away in the ocean. The instructor and I swam to the ocean bottom. We saw colorful corals and all types of magnificent, exotic, colorful marine life. Thankfully, we sighted no sharks. At one point, I held out my hand to brush a sea urchin. Different and weird, and fortunately harmless, as many urchins are venomous. But I did it!

Once back on the beach, I came to understand the phrase "the world is your oyster." I had never pictured myself in Hawaii, let alone scuba diving in the ocean. To think that it all started with just struggling through a few laps in a community pool. I was proud of myself for not allowing my age, ethnicity, or other biases from my zip code story to hold me back from growing, learning, and living a better life.

CLASS MIGRANTS IN THE BUSINESS ENVIRONMENT

The fear of drowning in a pool can be compared to the same feeling class migrants get when they step into a business environment for the first time. Class-migrant personnel can sometimes feel that they are in an ocean with colossal waves knocking them off course and currents pulling them under. That feeling can be overcome but only with proper direction and strategy. The environment can feel intimidating to a class migrant—even after a few years, especially if management has not taken strides to mentor or guide the class migrant on the business or its practices and protocols.

Part of this management failure might be related to fear of offending a class migrant. Other times it can reflect the degree of awareness of cultural differences in backgrounds; hence, the reason for this book and the need for guidance. It's commonplace for most of us to assume that those with whom we work have had similar upbringings and understand the same social experiences, norms, and business protocols. And in situations where it's evident that employees do not have the same experiences, the class migrant can feel alienated, and interactions can feel awkward for all parties.

Feeling awkward takes me back to my mechanical engineering days on K Street when my coworkers shared their different vacation experiences to Europe, Asia, Australia, and Africa, and then asked, "How about you, Chris?" After I reluctantly mentioned my visit to Florida as a child, the conversation ended abruptly.

These communication and social challenges also remind me of the woman I met at the pool who felt it necessary to explain her "poor" swimming performance, which was implied when she stated that she wasn't feeling like herself, so she only did seventy laps. In her mind, everyone, including me, knew that seventy laps was not up to par for an advanced swimmer who can swim twice that far, unbeknownst to me at the time. In the face of her subjectivity or performance issues, she hadn't noticed that I was struggling with a mere three laps. All too well, this shows us that people are not aware of others in their immediate environment. It also intimates that each of us fears what other people think of us or expect from us.

It boggles the mind to think that humans communicate their understanding through a simple nod of the head, as I did to the woman at the pool, when, in reality, we can't relate or understand what the issue is at all. That is, when the woman made excuses for her performance, she must have assumed that I was judging her. If she had been aware that I was struggling with fears of drowning and could barely swim three laps, she likely would not have mentioned her failure at seventy laps. Ironically, while on different rungs of the swimming ladder, we were both embarrassed about our performance. Little did she realize that her "failed performance" was so impressive—it inspired me to up my game and become the swimmer that I am today.

This example shows us, first, that you can expand your zip code story by challenging your biases. Second, it's an example for those who don't understand why people with different zip code stories struggle when they experience new cultures. And finally, it gives insight into all the biases and mental hurdles class migrants must overcome in order to succeed in new zip codes.

5

Ten Things Managers and Class Migrants Need to Know

The best investment you can make is in yourself . . . the more you learn, the more you'll earn. —Warren Buffett

When I first walked through the doors of Cook Ross, a consulting firm that drives inclusive leadership and culture, the foliage wall behind the reception desk displayed two strange words that changed my life: "Inner Work." What does inner work have to do with company values? At the time, that's what I was asking because most companies feature values such as integrity, team building, leadership, and performance. Not Inner Work. "In order to do the kind of work we do," Howard Ross, founder of Cook Ross, said, "you must do your inner work."[1]

Iyanla Vanzant, lawyer, inspirational speaker, author, and life coach, talks about the importance of developing the mind, spirit, emotions, and body. These building blocks "determine how you see yourself . . . how you show up in the world . . . how you experience the world . . . and how the world responds to you."[2] Iyanla's four cornerstones help define inner work, where each brick represents "who you are," which is what Ross meant about inner work.

1. Engage in Inner Work for Personal Development

Inner work is one of the hardest things to do because it requires self-exploration, discovering your unknowns, and analyzing your past, your fears, and your pain points. It requires you to confront the enemy within. To illustrate what inner work looks like, it's helpful to reflect on the legendary movie *Star Wars: A New Hope*. Inner work, also called shadow work, begins by entering a cave, like the dark cave Yoda instructed his mentee, Jedi, to enter. When Luke Skywalker asks Yoda, "What's in the cave?" Yoda answers, "Only what you take with you."

Skywalker walks into the cave and his arch-nemesis, Darth Vader, confronts him. Skywalker draws his lifesaver and fights Vader. Eventually, Skywalker strikes Vader's helmet, and his head comes off. When Skywalker looks down, he sees his face inside the helmet—not Darth Vader. This was a significant scene in the movie because Skywalker's face in Darth Vader's helmet represents his own fears and truths about himself. When people do inner work, they're much like Skywalker when he enters a dark cave. The only thing they bring with them is themselves. There's no one else to blame or fight but your own inner fears.

> Your visions will become clear only when you can look into your own heart. Who looks outside, dreams; who looks inside, awakes.[3] —C. G. Jung

It's easy to blame others for our problems and pain in life. Many people blame their position on their bosses, jobs, friends, and family. The truth is, every adult is responsible for her own development and position, but many don't take responsibility for it.

In my mid-twenties, I blamed a lot of my challenges and misfortunes on my parents. I thought, if only my parents were more successful, I wouldn't have all these problems. I couldn't see it at that time, but it wasn't true. Considering their zip code stories, my parents did an excellent job raising my sister and me, especially with what they knew. Although they helped to shape my formative years, they are not to blame. I needed to continue my growth and uncover my biases so that I could see the truth.

THE FIRST INNER-WORK STEPS TO PRACTICE DAILY

By blaming myself and others, I imprisoned myself. I wasn't free until I became serious about inner work. Self-discovery is not easy. It requires you to face your worst thoughts, fears, and feelings, and resist the urge to rationalize or ignore the notions that emanate from your conscious mind. Each person needs to pinpoint the thoughts that have convinced him that he is inadequate, unworthy, or unimportant. The idea is to give yourself and others a second chance and forgive yourself so that you can forgive others.

To forgive yourself, you need first to identify your anger, pain points, and the negative feelings that you carry around in life like gospel. But they're not gospel, only a narrative that you developed over time—the only narrative you could make sense of at those critical moments in your life. We also need to remember that social class does not define our worth; only you determine your worth. Every person, including our parents, did the best they could with the support and knowledge that they had.

> Social class has nothing to do with the person's worth. —Howard Ross

THE SECOND INNER-WORK STEPS TO PRACTICE DAILY

The second step is to allow your mind to travel back in time. Look at yourself as an innocent child; talk to that rebellious, angry, or wounded teenager who lives within—or that young adult who sees the world as a battlefield, then console and mentor that child.

Again, as the adult you are today, look at yourself as a child—as you would look at your own child, niece, or nephew who is suffering or feeling the pain you feel or have felt. Picture yourself kneeling at that child's level. Ask that child how he feels, listen to his reply, acknowledge those feelings, show empathy, and say that you understand. Now envision yourself comforting that child. Scoop up that child or place your hand on his shoulder. Now validate and convince that child by saying, "No matter what you've done, it doesn't make you a bad person. Those negative thoughts are not true. They're merely thoughts that helped you cope, the only way you knew how." Tell your inner child:

I understand how you feel. It's OK to feel that way. But you cannot blame yourself for the past or something that you once had no
control over. You did what you did, said what you said, and acted
the way you acted—because you didn't know better—because no
one was able to show you how to cope. No one knew how to show
you how to love yourself. You didn't have the support, information,
and knowledge that you needed. I am here now. I am here for you
always, and we will work on this together. I love you, and we'll talk
again tomorrow.

Feeling unworthy, unloved, stupid, or useless did not happen overnight; it's a long-held (false) belief that you deduced based on what
you knew at the time. Be patient with yourself; it will take time to
recall your inner innocence and beauty, to reengineer new thought
patterns and good beliefs about yourself. It's a process with ebbs
and flows of progress.

As I went through this process, I began to realize that as an adult,
no one is left to blame—not even myself. I was then able to take full
responsibility for my actions moving forward, and I could forgive
myself and forgive those I believed harmed me in the past. Inner
work allowed me to grow in so many areas of my life, especially in
my relationships.

Once I took ownership of my actions, I stopped making excuses
and quit blaming others. Although this is important for everyone,
it's critical for class migrants. Class migrants, like all other human
beings, find ways to protect themselves from pain. They become
defensive. They not only tend to blame others for their problems,
but they also carry an extraordinary amount of self-guilt, self-doubt,
and self-blame. Undoing this defense mode and its destructive path
is what inner work is all about. It will change "how you see yourself . . . how you show up in the world . . . how you experience the
world . . . and how the world responds to you."[4]

If we carry our past into every situation, we will remain in the
past and in the same position. But once we take ownership, we can
then become vulnerable. That may sound counterproductive, but
once you become vulnerable, amazing things begin to unfold. You
not only feel safe to reach out for help, but others will offer help
because they'll sense that you're open to receiving it. Vulnerability
is like a superpower because it enables you to build healthier relationships with those from any zip code. And that's when the magic
happens! Suddenly, you're no longer looking for someone to blame,

not even yourself. You show up more confident, not because you know all the answers or have more money, education, or cultural experiences. You show up confident because you no longer wear the mask of self-doubt. Absent self-doubt, you're willing to take more risks and gain more rewards in return.

THE THIRD INNER-WORK STEPS TO PRACTICE DAILY

When my girls were younger, we attended the Unity Center, a contemporary Christian and spiritual church. One Sunday, Reverend Sylvia gave a sermon about meditation. She said it is the way to success and prosperity. That comment made me angry. Up to that point, I had believed that money—cold, hard cash—would be the answer to my problems. It didn't occur to me at first, but I soon realized that no matter how much money I earned, it never solved my issues or changed my position in life. Money only reflected my own problems. Owning a nice car or watch doesn't change who you are. Spending beyond your means and buying expensive clothing doesn't set you up for success. Some people try to cure or cover their problems by shopping or rearranging their furniture. None of that can complete you or prepare you for your future.

Meditation helped me understand this. About a year after speaking to the reverend, I finally tried meditation. It took everything I had because I was not used to quieting my mind and being physically still for any length of time. Eventually, I attended a meditation session in Owings Mills, Maryland, which I found online by searching for meditation groups. Once a week, eight to ten people gathered in a small office to meditate.

When I first arrived, my bias radar buzzed so loudly that I could barely concentrate. The people in the meditation class looked weird to me. One lady kept humming and looking around the room; it looked strange and shady to me. Another guy had cat hair plastered all over his clothing. I wondered if this was for me. After thirty minutes or so, I caught myself judging. I was judging the people, the practice, the building—you name it. Then I realized that they might be judging me, too. It also dawned on me that I was projecting my thoughts. In other words, because I *perceived* that they were judging me, I judged them. Maybe the humming did it, but realizing this humbled me.

From that point on, I stopped judging and, miraculously, I stopped seeing everyone as a threat. We are all at different points on our journey, but we are all on the same plane; everybody is just trying to be the best they can be—given what they know. Being aware of this allows me not to take things personally. The goal was to keep my mind open, which couldn't occur if I judged people. I wasn't about to step on my own toes; I knew that meditation was powerful, and I was told many times it was the key to success. If daily meditation helped the late Kobe Bryant and helps Michael Jordan, Will Smith, Katy Perry, Paul McCartney, and Oprah Winfrey, it can help you.

Once settled in, the instructor had the group gather in a circle on the floor. She then opened with an icebreaker by sharing her personal story of how she entered meditation practice. After a serious relationship had ended, she experienced a profound loss and emptiness, a depression that led her to attempt suicide. While recovering from her suicide attempt, someone recommended a silent retreat. Figuring that she had nothing to lose, she tried it. She quickly learned how to meditate and the benefits of a quiet mind.

She then spoke about the five brain waves: delta, theta, alpha, beta, and gamma. Now, this intrigued me, because it's more than just humming and sitting still with your legs crossed—proven science is behind meditation. Knowing that took the weirdness and social stigma away from the whole idea of, especially for a Black man engaging in meditation. Today, there are numerous close, affordable, and culturally sensitive meditation spaces, both online and offline.[5] There is no shame in improving yourself. If you don't do it for yourself, who will?

The meditation teacher also touched on the ancient practice of yoga and daily self-affirmations—giving yourself gratitude, praise, and a pat on the back each night before bed. These exercises help you achieve mindfulness and the inner work needed to increase peace, patience, and self-love and decrease fears, anger, stress, and anxiety.

The meditation instructor told us that it would not take long for beginners to notice a difference (internally and externally). I wasn't sure what to think about her promise, but I promised myself I'd remain open.

After meditating with the group and on my own for three weeks, I noticed that I didn't get as frustrated with every minor hiccup or bump in the road. And when I did, I didn't react impulsively or become infuriated. I also became more self-aware. I was able to be present and live in the moment.

About six weeks into my meditation sessions, I opened my apartment door and walked in as usual. Only it was unusual. It felt like the first time I had been there. The whole place seemed dim and drab. Something was missing. I stood there and looked around. Then I realized that some of the bulbs and the light fixtures needed to be replaced. Until that moment, I had never noticed that my apartment was so dismal. Once I replaced the burned-out bulbs, the apartment perked up. And just like that, I started to see life through a brighter lens. After meditating for a few months, I began to develop a heightened sense of mindfulness. Mindfulness occurs when you reach a state of calm and can remain in that state. You learn how to do this by quieting your mind and paying attention to what's happening at the moment.

Mindfulness allowed me to sort out things in my brain. My mind tends to race, but when I'm in a mindful state, things slow down, come into focus, and I can pinpoint how I feel, why, and what I need to do about it. Meditation calms your mind, body, and emotions. Before meditating, just thinking about everything happening in my life would have made me react before thinking things through—this was groundbreaking. It allowed me to plan and strategize before making a decision, which has helped me in all areas of life. It led me out of a dead-end relationship and a dead-end job.

Meditation has been a powerful tool for inner work. But I've incorporated an array of personal development tools to grow. I read self-help books, work with coaches and mentors, engage in spiritual practices, journal, and develop relationships with those who hold me accountable. Each year I set a goal to engage in a personal development program. Every successful person I know involves himself in inner work or personal development. Each person has preferences; you must choose the personal development tools that are best for you, ones you know you will commit to using daily, and ones that will allow you to do the inner work and grow to your fullest potential.

2. Develop New Relationships
Many of the personal development books I've read say that your five closest relationships will determine your success in life. One

of my favorites is *Think and Grow Rich* by Napoleon Hill. Although making new friends once you are in your mid-twenties can be difficult, it is necessary for growth.

In 2015, I worked for New York Life, a financial services company. On my first day there, I met a guy named Eddie. Something about Eddie was different. He didn't dress or speak like the rest of my coworkers. And he always seemed to think outside the box. One day, Eddie and I were on a break, and I mentioned the names of a few cars that I like. He said, "Oh, cars are nice, but what about boats?"[6] At that point in my life, I had never considered driving or steering a boat. Later, I learned that he was a member of a yacht club. Because Eddie's zip code story was different from mine, every conversation expanded my story.

One day while we were having lunch, Eddie answered the phone, and out of the blue he started speaking fluent Italian. It blew my mind because Eddie was African American, from the inner city of Baltimore. Then I discovered that he had lived in Italy for quite a while and had two children. The more time I spent with Eddie, the more my zip code story broadened. My association with Eddie made me look at my life differently. I learned a lot from Eddie. Sometimes, we limit ourselves because we cannot envision ourselves in a particular place or see ourselves doing something we have never done before. In a way, we stereotype ourselves. If Eddie could speak two languages, then there was no reason I couldn't speak two languages, too. So, I took a Spanish class, which I'd always wanted to do but always put off.

Developing new relationships has been critical to my personal and professional growth. Currently, I have three mentors who help me grow in different areas of my life. Relationships with my fellow consultants nourish me and support my career growth. The relationships I've built over my lifetime have always helped me, but just in a different way.

One year ago, I started a group with two Jewish guys, both almost fifteen years younger than I am. Our zip code stories are pretty different. Both have wives and are in their twenties with no kids, and I am forty-five, divorced with two kids in college—but we learn from one another. We meet once a week on an accountability call and every three months in person to have fun. Although we have different backgrounds, we have one common goal: to hold each other accountable for the goals that we've set. We have built a strong brotherhood. It doesn't matter if you develop new relationships with old friends or put yourself in an environment and state of mind to meet new friends. Whoever you spend time with consistently will influence you. So, think about building relationships with people who want what you want out of life.

3. Try New Cultural Activities

Trying different cultural activities has opened my eyes to how other cultures live and work. Engaging in conversations and activities with other cultures helps me expand my zip code story. I've experienced different cultures by attending weddings and birthday parties, community events, eating at ethnic restaurants, and traveling. I'll discuss travel in the next section. The important thing here is to seek opportunities and take advantage of all invitations, especially if they involve different cultural backgrounds.

My daughter Lauren loves Korean culture, so much so that she started to learn about Korean culture by watching Korean soap operas and practicing the Korean language with her friends. One day, she asked me to go to a Korean restaurant with her. I was a little uneasy about walking right in and finding our own seat—and then came the menu. Well, not really; the menu was on the wall. My food bias was alerted when our waiter served us banchan, or groups of bright-colored side dishes. It was visually appealing but odd. I didn't get a plate of octopus tentacles or roasted silkworm, but I wasn't used to their look or taste. I tried everything but primarily stuck to the grilled chicken, rice, and pickles.

> In studying other cultures, we learn more about ourselves and our relationship to all things in this world. —Eustace Conway

The cuisine may not have been to my liking, but I thought it was a great way to spend time with my daughter, do something that she likes to do, and learn about Korean culture. While there, I noticed that Koreans take great pride in the way the food is prepared and presented. Korean food symbolizes Korean culture. An ancient Korean proverb says, "What looks good tastes good." I'm looking forward to trying more Korean dishes to acquire a taste for it.[7] The restaurant was filled with chatter and laughter, and we grilled our food at our table. What is cool about Korean dining is the sharing of food. Unlike wolfing down a $10 hamburger, it's a bonding experience of eating and sharing, reflecting the communal nature of the culture.

My daughter's fetish with Korean culture extends beyond mine. She loves K-pop, which is Korean hip-hop. We have also attended Korean community events. And Lauren plans to travel to Korea in the next two years. She's excited, and I'm excited for her to have the whole cultural experience.

Experiencing a new culture has expanded my daughter's zip code story. Being bilingual is an advantage both in Korea and the United States. It has many cognitive benefits, but it also makes you more competitive in the job market. Bilingualism allows you to communicate with different cultures and attract new leads to the products and services a company offers. When my nineteen-year-old interviews for a job and says she can speak two languages, it gives her a leg up. Plus, people are less likely to stereotype her as a typical African American teenager. Doing things outside her own culture does not mean that she forgets it; it just means that she has an expanded zip code story, which helps her relate to more than one culture.

4. Travel, Travel, Travel

Traveling has opened my eyes more than the books I have read or any other experiences. Direct experience with different environments, cultures, foods, and languages ultimately changes your perspective in life. I've traveled across the United States, visited eight different countries and two continents, all within three years. Traveling was not a big part of my life until I met my fiancée, Kerryann, and decided to become a contract trainer. Kerryann loves to travel. She was responsible for my first international trip to Jamaica, her place of birth. Once I became a contract trainer for Fred Pryor, founding chair of Fred Pryor Seminars, I immediately became a national speaker, allowing me to see most of the country. All of this occurred after I was forty. Before this, I developed myself personally and professionally, which prepared me to take on such a role.

Although our trip to Kerryann's native country required me to obtain a passport, I wish I would have gotten my passport at a younger age. At times in my life I had thought of traveling, and I might have if I had not had the obstacle of the four-week waiting period to obtain the passport.

Failing to take this step is a tragedy for many people. Many don't take the initiative to get a passport because they think traveling abroad is out of reach. They also hold themselves back because they don't have a community of people to support their travel or believe it's unaffordable.

Nowadays, although the pandemic has curtailed traveling to a degree, most of my colleagues and friends travel internationally regularly. Kerryann and I recently purchased airplane tickets to Puerto Rico for $150. For some people, coming up with $150 for anything is a challenge. Others will spend $150 on a pair of shoes and not think twice. Kerryann and I spend money on what we value and what's now a part of our new zip code story. If the latest Jordans are valued in your zip code story, that's what you will spend your money on. But if personal and professional growth is what you desire, then you'll put your money elsewhere. The more I travel, the more I meet people from different cultures and the more my personal and professional zip code story expands.

5. Interview Others Who Were Brought Up Differently Than You

I love meeting new people and asking them about their life. I have always been curious about how people came to be who they are and what makes them tick. Sometimes I meet people in transit who I'll never see again. Other times, I meet people, and we establish personal or working relationships. People tend to gravitate toward those they are familiar with and enjoy sharing things in common, which is great, but it keeps them in their comfort zone. I've always been interested in people who are different from me and now know that it's essential to meet others who differ. Whoever I meet, I look at it as an inquiry. I want to understand their zip code story and their likes and dislikes. It's not just about what they might be able to do for you; people like it when you take a genuine interest in them and their lives. Developing interviewing skills has benefited my career and personal life.

Inquiring is not a fool's errand; it's an errand to prevent foolishness.

Many years ago, on a flight home from Kansas City, I sat next to an older gentleman who was wearing socks and sandals. I've never understood why people wear socks with sandals. I couldn't get it off my mind. Although I was tired, I wanted to know what type of guy wears socks and sandals. The conversation felt a little awkward, but after speaking with this gentleman for a few minutes, I learned that he had a fascinating life story, and he was in the same career field that I was pursuing. He seemed to enjoy answering my questions. Toward the end of our flight, I asked him if I could contact him later to continue our conversation. He agreed. Soon after, I asked him to be my mentor because he had a wealth of experience and wisdom in the leadership consulting field. That was more than two years ago. Since then, we've become close and meet every month.

To clarify, when I say interview others, I do not mean to drill them. I mean, get to know them by asking casual questions. Never interrogate or ask a bunch of pre-scripted questions that will repel or make people feel like you're up to something.

A simple inquiry could lead to expanding your zip code story. The steps you take to learn about a different culture, such as making it a point to travel, making new friends, obtaining a new job, or finding a mentor, help you create a new future.

6. Seek a Mentor or Two

As I mentioned in chapter 1, my partner who ran a mentoring program used to say, "If you can't see it, you can't be it."[8] So although you may want to be CEO of a Fortune 500 company, if you've never talked to one, interviewed one, read one's book, or developed a relationship with one, your chances are slim to none of becoming one. This is not just a quote from my colleagues. It's true for every successful person in every area of life. If you don't believe me, find someone you consider to be successful—someone you know, an idol, or a stranger. I'm willing to bet that if you ask enough questions and do enough research, you'll find that successful people had a mentor or person who showed them how to succeed. They may not have called this person a mentor, and they may never have thought about how they got to where they are, but they had someone to guide them.

> Show me a successful individual and I'll show you someone who had real positive influences in his or her life. I don't care what you do for a living—if you do it well I'm sure someone was there cheering you on or showing the way. A mentor. —Denzel Washington

I have read the biographies of Barack Obama, Thomas Edison, Steve Jobs, Oprah Winfrey, Albert Einstein, Leonardo da Vinci, Arnold

Schwarzenegger, Martin Luther King Jr., and many more. Every story involved a mentor of sorts. They either met them in person, or they read their biography and applied the principles from those they wanted to emulate. Denzel Washington shares his personal story of the mentors who helped guide his life. The award-winning actor was so passionate about mentorship, he wrote a book titled *A Hand to Guide Me*. The book shared the stories of more than seventy leading personalities in American theater, sports, business, and politics. Each of them talked about mentorship and how it improved their lives.

> The delicate balance of mentoring someone is not creating them in your own image but giving them the opportunity to create themselves. —Steven Spielberg

Finding a mentor is one of the most important things that you can leverage for personal growth. All the information in the world is useless unless you know when and how to use it. A mentor can show you how to use the information you have learned, introduce you to people who can show you the ropes, reveal your blind spots, inspire you, hold you accountable, and ask you questions that open your mind. Don't be left behind because you are too afraid to ask. You don't need smarts or wisdom to start conversations and ask questions.

> A mentor is someone who allows you to see the hope inside yourself. —Oprah Winfrey

Mentors are usually people you admire and have achieved a certain level of success in a specific area. Because of their experiences in particular areas of life and business, they can save you years, tons of money, and lots of stress as you pursue your goals. Without a mentor, you're likely to become frustrated, give up, run out of time or money, derailing you from your goals and dreams. That used to be me. My guess is that it has been the case for you in business and life. If you're going to be successful, you need a mentor!

When I talk about mentorship, people always ask, "How do I find a mentor?" The answer is simple: look for one.

> Ask and it will be given to you; seek and you will find; knock and the door will be opened to you. —Matthew 7:7

Most people do not ask, seek, or knock, so the door stays shut. I am always looking for successful people from whom to learn, and somehow, they appear. When I attend an event with exceptional speakers, I make it a point to speak with them afterward. Then I ask for their card and follow up. I also ask if they have time for an interview. Most say yes if their schedules permit. After the interview, if I think they have expertise in something I want to learn, I will formally ask them to mentor me. Over the years, this strategy has led to many fruitful mentorships. From business owners to authors and millionaires, I have met and maintained several growth-oriented relationships. Staying curious and being mentored are invaluable because they expand your zip code story.

Asking someone to mentor you can feel intimidating because they are *and must be* more successful than you. One of the largest obstacles that class migrants face is learning how to be vulnerable, at least enough to ask questions. But you must be vulnerable for it to work. If you enter a mentorship thinking that mentor won't understand, he won't because you'll hold back, which means he'll never have a chance to understand you or guide you. You'll be pleasantly surprised to know that many mentors can understand because many of them have had firsthand experiences or have secondhand knowledge of stories similar to yours.

Our judgments of people are usually way off. One would never know it by looking at Howard Ross's Tesla, best-selling books, or successful business ownership, but he wasn't always wealthy. He was raised by parents who were neither educated nor wealthy. His father was intimate with the life, struggles, and emotions of the lower class.

Howard grew up in Washington, D.C., in the 1950s. Both of his parents came from families who owned small businesses that later had to close. Howard's father lost his father at the age of twelve, then fell into poverty, and he, his brother, and mother had to live with a relative in one ten-by-ten room.

Howard said, "My experience growing up was, I did not feel like we lacked anything, we were never food insecure. But we also did not waste any or have anything to waste. I remembered my parents cutting coupons, and my mother would go seemingly miles out of the way to save a couple of cents on a roll of toilet paper . . . unfortunately, because my father did not have any high school education, a lot of stuff was not available to him. My father was not a guy who lived his life as a victim. I do not want to give that impression. But he definitely had a sense of elitist snobs, people who thought they were better than him." On the other hand, Howard said, my father "was also somebody who, because of his life experience, had a particular sense of compassion for people who did not have . . . Even if he did not have much, he would find something. He would give a quarter, fifty cents, a dollar, or something. It was just like breathing for him to do that because he had been on the other side of that." In time, Howard's father became a manager at Pep Boys. "I would go down with him on weekends, a lot on Saturdays, and I would stay in the back with the guys who changed the tires, who were a rung below the guys in the store."

"In those days," Howard said, "the 1950s, late fifties probably, the guys in the store were white, and the guys who changed the tires were Black. That was the way it was set up, but I would hang out with those guys. My father said, 'Why don't you go up and help Wendell change the tires and make yourself useful?' There was no sense that 'No, we belong here.' It was like, get a feeling for what real work is; that was kind of my father's mind-set. It was like, make sure you get your hands dirty, know what real work is about. For my dad, it was very much like, "Look, not everybody is as lucky as you. See what it is like to do that.' He would encourage me to get jobs where I work with working people . . . He really understood that, and that has definitely shaped my values."[9]

People who have worked their way to the top are typically happy and willing to help others. Howard is one of those people. He has spent his life mentoring and going to bat for others. He also understands the internal challenges that class migrants face.

"One of the things I would say to people who are class migrants is that class, like any other divisions we talked about, gets established in an inside-outside way," Howard said. "There is the in-group, and there is the out-group, and the in-group obviously are the people who are wealthier, right? But whenever we have in-group, out-group, you have that dynamic of what's been called the 'out-group homogeneity effect.' You tend to think of them as all the same. So, it is like wealthy people think of poor people as being kind of all the same and poor people think of wealthy people as kind of being all the same. And so, a lot of times people will come up to somebody like me, and they see me to a later stage of my career after I built this big company, and I got fifty people working for me, and I am driving a Tesla, and all this stuff, and they think, well, you will never understand what my life was about. Whereas the truth is, I may very well understand it because of my life experience, my father's life experience, because of the other people I have worked with within communities that were really underserved and under-resourced. As a result of that, sometimes people did not come to me for the kind of support that I could provide them because they were afraid that I would be looking down on them."[10]

I was fortunate to meet Howard and to have been mentored by him. Although no one is like Howard, many people are capable of mentoring. And, usually, people are flattered when you ask them to be your mentor.

Willie Jolly, an international motivational speaker, was also my mentor and provided me with a lot of helpful advice. Years ago, he gave me the strategy, insights, and support to start my speaking business. I formed another mentorship with a business owner, who, at the time, gave me one of my very first training contracts. My most recent mentor wrote a professional letter on my behalf, which aided me in landing a rare consulting position. Mentorship, quite literary, was a springboard to my career. Although finding a mentor can be a challenge, it's one you must overcome, as mentors are critical to your success in business and life.

7. Increase Your Level of Education

Increasing your level of education can open doors. College is not for everyone, so I am not suggesting that you go back to formal school unless it aligns with your goals. On the other hand, a degree, certification, or specialized training can qualify you for opportunities that are currently outside your reach. For the purposes of this book, I refer to two types of education.

The first is formal education. Formal education involves a certificate or diploma from an accredited school such as a college, trade school, association, or well-known institution. When I decided to switch careers, I only had a high-school education. Once I decided on the career that interested me, I took certification classes. Although I did not have a degree, the certifications helped me gain entrance into a different industry without direct work experience. Once I decided to earn my bachelor's degree in organizational management, it aided me in landing a consulting position.

The second type is informal education, which requires you to read books, take noncredit classes at your local library or community college, gain work experience, and interview thought leaders in the industry you are pursuing. Whether formal or informal, education can broaden your horizons, make your résumé stand out, and unlock doors for you.

8. Volunteer

Volunteer work is rewarding and can expand your zip code story. You have so many ways to give back. Volunteering is beneficial to your personal and professional growth. Many people and religious organizations volunteer their time as missionaries, which allows them to travel to different parts of the world. Typically, nonprofits offer volunteer opportunities that align with their mission. Schools also provide volunteer opportunities to work with students in various capacities. When you choose to volunteer, you have a chance to give back and learn about people from different walks of life.

> Life's most urgent question is: What are you doing for others?
> —Martin Luther King Jr.

Over the years, volunteering has led me to encounter people I otherwise would not have met. Chris Tucker, Taraji P. Henson, Louis Gossett Jr., BeBe Winans, and my movie star crush, Angela Bassett, are just a few people I have had the privilege of meeting. However, there was one volunteer event that I regret not participating in because I missed the opportunity to meet President Barack Obama and his family.

Each year, on the third Monday in January, community-based programs, schools, libraries, and other outreach programs honor Martin Luther King Jr. by providing a day of volunteer service. The celebrities from the same program I'm involved with hosted a day of service that I did not attend because of a conflict in my schedule—big mistake. The moral of the story is, if you volunteer your time, you might have the opportunity to meet the president of the United States.

My volunteer experiences range from sitting on the board of a nonprofit for ten years, mentoring young people for seventeen years, building houses for Habitat for Humanity, hosting parent workshops for inner-city schools, providing employment readiness workshops for my church, and providing personal development workshops for inmates in a jail. Each volunteer experience has helped me expand my zip code story and provided me with invaluable work experience.

9. Do Things That Make You Feel Uncomfortable

Most people avoid situations in which they feel uncomfortable or awkward. That's why we avoid difficult conversations, making eye contact with strangers, going to the gym, or sitting on an airplane next to children. Unfortunately, growth doesn't happen without discomfort. When you're learning something new, you make mistakes. When you make mistakes, you learn. If you keep trying and working on a skill, you eventually grow and develop new skills. In turn, this expands your zip code story.

Troy Brown, an African American, Baltimore native, and Harvard Law School graduate, discusses why it's challenging but essential to get out of your comfort zone, explore different places, meet different people, and try different things.

> That fear of newness, that fear of change, the absurdity of things—saying "I do not like it" when you have never tried it is something that often does not fully go away. No matter how much you make sure, no matter how much you grow, there is some element that still wants to hold us back from change. Our brains do not change quickly. It typically takes some slow evolution for change. So, . . . my advice to class migrants is to stay hungry and do not be afraid of newness. Something ceases [sic] within us when we close our minds off to newness and change.
>
> If I or any of us succumbed as a kid to that taunt of you are acting White, or maybe I should not read as much, or maybe I should not participate as much in class or let me start a fight with a kid because that is what Black kids do, we are trapped. If I had succumbed to that kind of foolishness, then something within me, the thinker of a student, the professor, the Mason lawyer in me, would have starved to death. I would not have fed myself with that new food of growth of reading, of change, of doing new things, meeting new people, testing our limits. If you are a class migrant, there is that thought of "stay with your own. Stay with your group. Stay within what is known. Do not leave this pond and explore the ocean." It is a part of our safety mechanism, I think. There are good and legitimate reasons why that instinct has developed and has not been wiped out of us over thousands of years. It is safe not to grow [sic] and stay what you are, but there is a danger in it too because if you do not change and grow, then part of you dies. You do not fully actualize.

I think when it comes to class migrants [sic], I'd say, do not be afraid to tell your familiar pond, I am not leaving you, but I am looking to explore—and if you are afraid of my growth, then you have left the pond, not me. Do not be afraid to challenge old ideas . . . challenge old traditions. Remember them. Question why they are there but do not be afraid to challenge them. Because migration, by its very definition, means you are moving. You have got to be on the move.

I would definitely encourage [sic] everyone to travel. Whether it is a whole bunch of different cities or one, stay there for a while, immerse yourself—definitely save up for that. If that is difficult, reading is one of the most effective ways to really transport yourself, not just geographically, geopolitically, chronologically; you can take yourself anywhere, even inside the mind of another person. There is nothing more important than reading. (Troy Brown, interview by author, "Why it's challenging but essential to get out of your comfort zone, explore different places, meet different people, and try different things," n.d.)

> Do one thing every day that scares you. Those small things that make us uncomfortable help us build courage to do the work we do. —Eleanor Roosevelt

The great thing about getting outside your comfort zone in one area of life is that it allows you to apply what you have learned in many other areas. I've walked out, been pushed out, and pulled out of my comfort zone numerous times. When I went skydiving, the instructor strapped to my back pushed me out of the plane. One time I went scuba diving, and my instructor had to keep telling me, "You're not going to get eaten by Jaws," or something to that effect. My most uncomfortable and awkward moments were my first few speaking engagements. No, make that my first twenty or thirty speaking engagements. During one of my engagements, I was so nervous I spilled a bottle of water on my suit while trying to take a sip. Talk about out of my comfort zone! Today, as an international speaker, I'm proud of myself and thankful that I worked through the discomfort and awkwardness—they were worth every minute.

You don't have to jump out of an airplane, swim with sharks, stand onstage, or talk to hundreds of strangers, but you do have to get out of your comfort zone if you plan to grow in your personal and professional life. You can always start small by talking to someone you don't know, asking out someone different on a date, or signing up for karaoke. Just commit to doing something that moves you out of your comfort zone so you can experience the growth necessary to expand your zip code story.

10. Increase Your Empathy for Yourself and Others

> Empathy fuels connection; sympathy drives disconnection.[11] — Brené Brown

To fully understand a person with a different zip code story, you must have empathy. Empathy is the ability to understand what someone else is feeling and why. Whether it's a personal or professional relationship, the inability to empathize with another person will prevent your relationships from growing and thriving. Empathy is more than simply inquiring and hearing what someone has to say; when people feel like you are interested and understand them on an emotional level, trust flourishes. When trust flourishes, communication increases, and your relationships become authentic. People cherish genuine relationships because they hold you accountable, tell you the truth, make you laugh, and support your growth. Increasing your empathy correlates with expanding your zip code story.

When I worked for the Maryland Department of Juvenile Services, I was assigned to one of the youth correctional facilities. During my time there, a conflict occurred between the principal of the juvenile school and some of the teachers. I could not believe that the adults responsible for teaching the kids were acting like children themselves. On one occasion, while the principal was speaking during our staff meeting, a teacher threw a piece of paper right at her. Another time, the teachers went on an unofficial strike, which means that they failed to teach their students, disrupting their learning. Although this wouldn't be a major problem in a regular school, it could have led to a breach in security there.

A week after I started my position as a teacher specialist, a few teachers told me not to trust the school principal. That same week, the principal told me not to trust the disgruntled teachers. I was caught between a "rock and a hard place." I wanted to have a good relationship with my boss and supervisor; after all, they hired me and would be responsible for my performance evaluations. On the other hand, I also wanted to have good relations with my coworkers. Support is essential in any job, especially in a correctional facility.

If you are a teacher, you not only want but need support from your co-teachers because of hazards there, such as being assaulted by a juvenile inmate or having a riot erupt in your classroom, as it did during my tenure. When these life-threatening situations occur, you want to make sure you have the full support of your staff. For me, it meant that I needed to build relationships with my co-teachers as well as the principal. It was a challenge because of the volatile nature of the work environment, and the passive-aggressive behavior of the teachers and the principal did not help matters.

The nature of the situation left me no choice but to find a way to build relationships with both sides. I started with the principal. I met with her multiple times to try to understand her pain points. At the top of her list, as you can imagine, were a couple of teachers she deemed troublemakers. I did not take sides; instead, I had an authentic, assertive conversation to advise her that they may be troublemakers, but I also must work with them for safety reasons. I also told her that it was important as a new teacher there for me to build relationships with the teachers because it would help me build relationships with the students. I said, in the end, everyone, including the students, will have a better experience. She was not confident about my approach with the teachers, but I didn't give her any choice. She knew that I could not exclude myself from their activities, although she was aware that the activities included side-bar conversations about boycotts and passive-aggressive behavior toward her.

When I met with the teachers, they held nothing back. They verbally attacked the principal and told me how awful she was as a principal. I told them that I understood their perspective. I also told them nearly the same thing I said to the principal: "I need it to work with the principal because I am new, she is my boss, and I need to build a trusting relationship to support my integration into the school." They told me not to believe anything she said because she was a liar. Again, I thought it was odd that professionals were acting like children. But it was happening, so I made my position known. Quickly and assertively, I told the teachers that I planned to work with each of them and the principal, and I would not take sides.

At first, they were leery, but soon they respected my position. I assured them that I would keep their plans and information confidential and only discuss what was necessary to teach and run the school effectively. When I said this, the leader stared directly into my eyes to see if I was being truthful. I didn't blink or look away. I wanted him to know that I was a man of my word and that I had integrity. After his stare down, he reached out, and we shook hands. It was a good sign. When he extended his trust to me, so did the rest of the teachers.

After my conversations with the teachers and the principal, both began to confide in me. They spoke about the challenges they faced in the school, with each other, and even in their personal lives. The principal shared her desire to become the district superintendent, but she was frustrated with the overall administration of the department. It was clear she needed to improve her communication and community relations skills. The teachers shared their personal and professional aspirations as well. Both sides knew I was communicating with the other, but they trusted me and respected me because I told them where I stood early in our relationships.

This had a positive impact. However, the feuds continued. As the holiday season approached, no one was interested in preparing for a staff party. To help things along, I offered to dress up as Santa Claus, but I made my offer contingent: both parties had to agree to come to the party. One staff member laughed and said, "I'll come just to see that." He did, and so did everyone else. The event was a hit! Everyone had a great time, including the correctional officers. The success of this one event made all my efforts worthwhile. It increased my influence and my value at work. People started hearing that I was the go-to guy to get things done—all because I developed empathy for both parties without taking sides.

After the holiday party, both sides were OK with me communicating and having private meetings with the other side. I think they extended a high level of trust in me because I kept my word and helped each party understand the other's point of view. Although I wish the principal and the teachers had worked things out for the sake of the students, my ability to navigate these challenging relationships and stay safe while doing my job was a feat in itself. And it required me to exercise emotional intelligence and empathy for all involved.

Emotional intelligence is the ability to be aware of your emotions (how you feel and why) and the emotions of others (how they feel and why). This allows you not only to be aware of your emotions but also will enable you to empathize with others. It is impossible to have emotional intelligence without empathy, and vice versa.

Leadership success calls for 15 percent technical skills and 85 percent emotional intelligence. Astounding! More interesting, an article from the Harvard Division of Continuing Education states, "Emotional intelligence—the ability to, for instance, understand your effect on others and manage yourself accordingly—accounts for nearly 90 percent of what moves people up the ladder when IQ and technical skills are roughly similar."[12]

The moral of this story: empathy is necessary to understand the point of view of others. Whatever your zip code, you must be aware that it shapes how you see others. In contrast, others' zip code stories shape the way they see you. Empathy asks you to take a moment and consider the emotions of others and how their story impacts them and impacts you. It increases emotional intelligence and allows you to build relationships with those who have vastly different zip code stories from yours. In turn, building relationships enable you to increase your influence in the workplace and grow your dreams and your career.

> Empathy is not sympathy. Sympathy is a form of agreement. Empathy is not agreeing with someone; it is fully, deeply understanding that person, emotionally as well as intellectually.
> —Stephen R. Covey

One thing to keep in mind: it's not good enough to have empathy for others; you must also have sympathy for yourself. Too often, class migrants beat themselves up or put themselves down because they don't feel like they're good enough. I know this is true because I've seen others do it, but I have been guilty, too.

For most of my career, outside of engineering, I have not felt worthy of the positions I've held. I felt like I didn't measure up to my coworkers and sometimes to my friends. I thought others were better because of their education, two-parent household, happy marriages, nicer clothes, more money, bigger houses, or other stories that I made up in my head. These stories were probably not true, but I believed them. Comparing yourself to others is instinctual but of little use because it does nothing to help you write your new story.

I could not let go of my old story until I became more sympathetic to myself and empathetic with others. This was key to my personal development. Once I understood, my new story accelerated and expanded my zip code to national and international recognition for my work as a consultant. These ten building blocks will help you "determine how you see yourself . . . how you show up in the world . . . how you experience the world . . . and how the world responds to you."[13]

6

How Businesses Can Incorporate Social Class into Their Inclusion, Diversity, Equity, and Accessibility Initiatives

We should know that diversity makes for a rich tapestry, and we must understand that all the threads of the tapestry are equal in value no matter what their color. —Maya Angelou

This chapter shares some practical strategies that organizations can implement to support class migrants in their IDEA initiatives.

During the 1980s and 1990s, organizational initiatives focused on diversity training; then, sometime between the 1990s and the early 2000s, we began to hear the term diversity education. So, although I've been a corporate trainer for eighteen years, diversity and inclusion were the key terms when I entered the industry two years ago.

Today, some companies have broadened the scope to Inclusion Diversity Equity and Accessibility (IDEA). Others have only gotten as far as DE&I or Diversity, Equity, and Inclusion or some combination of this acronym.

Workplace diversity is not a new concept. The term has been around since the 1960s. But, for most companies, its implementation is another story. That is, according to McKinsey & Co., "Companies spend $8 billion a year on diversity training, but experts say these organizations have little to show for it."[1]

IDEA is a newer workplace model. Large corporations earmark hundreds of millions of dollars for IDEA initiatives; some have committees, others have hired a chief diversity officer. No matter how far along companies find themselves in their IDEA initiatives, one thing is for sure: the work is challenging. The lack of diverse people within an organization prevents it from having the talent needed to understand social class dynamics and, therefore, hampers effective IDEA education.

INCLUSION

Although diversity must occur first, inclusion is the most critical component of IDEA. Without inclusion, those with no voice—namely, class migrants—cannot be heard. One of my highly esteemed colleagues, Johnnetta B. Cole, PhD, said, "Diversity is like getting an invitation to the party. Inclusion is like getting asked to dance."[2] And "Belonging is when you get to choose the music,"[3] Howard Ross said.

Practitioners added inclusion to their diversity initiatives because they realized diversity isn't sustainable without inclusion. In other words, if you have a group of minority employees, and the company does not reflect an inclusive culture, employees will not feel included and therefore cannot thrive.

About six years ago, when I delivered time management training to a school board in Maryland, I asked participants how they could implement the time management skills they learned during the training. Ninety-five percent admitted that they could not execute their strategies because they had no control over their schedule.

Without any input from the staff, the school board had staggered the teachers' arrival times, which directly conflicted with employee productivity and work-life balance. To make matters worse, they asked me to show employees how to manage their time better, which further upset and irritated them.

Despite the board's efforts to solve the problem, they failed because they did not include employees in the decision making, so they could not see the challenges that the schedule presented for their employees.

By the time I came in, employees were frustrated and confused about why I was telling them to manage their time better. Had upper management included employees, they would have saved time and money by developing a new schedule that could work for everyone.

I see this problem in many companies. The manager or leader makes a decision that will severely affect employees but does not include them in the decision-making process. Unilateral leadership decisions prevent engagement and a sense of ownership in the outcome, decreasing motivation and retention.

This problem is even more unfavorable when it comes to diversity because people don't feel comfortable having awkward conversations about race, sexuality, gender, or religion. Further, they lack the experiences and the communication skills to handle such a conversation. The whole situation usually ends up messy. That's when they hire a consultant to fix things or at least tell them what they're doing wrong. I see this situation repeatedly, and it only breeds a culture of frustration and distrust.

It is more difficult in companies that have a large hierarchical organizational structure. Power dynamics within and between departments can stifle relationships and, therefore, snuff out inclusion initiatives. If a manager lacks emotional and cultural intelligence, she may exert positional authority, thinking that's where her power exists. Nothing could be further from the truth. Power lies in the ability to have an authentic, organic relationship with staff. When this occurs, it becomes second nature to get staff feedback and buy-in before making big decisions that negatively impact people and company culture. Inclusion allows for feedback, transparency, buy-in, collaboration, and innovation.

DIVERSITY

We all possess physical, emotional, and cognitive attributes and skills, backgrounds, educations, relationships, and experiences that make us unique. We call this diversity. If used properly, it can enrich company culture, expand zip code stories, resonate with the needs and wants of clients, and foster innovation.

Diversity, when properly harnessed, can bring about positive change in workplace culture and the culture of our society, which increases return on investment. Colin Kaepernick, a former NFL quarterback, believed that taking a knee during the national anthem would bring attention to racial injustice. His actions were an example of diversity of thought and personal values. Although Kaepernick's stance was controversial, it brought attention to injustice, which he is passionate about along with hundreds of thousands of other people. Unfortunately, his stand for injustice cost him his position for the San Francisco 49ers, but it created social awareness. For instance, Nike supported Colin's cause through its thirtieth anniversary of the "Just Do It!" campaign. He made a difference in the fight for social justice.

In a 2012 *Harvard Business Review* article "How Diversity Can Drive Innovation," authors Sylvia Ann Hewlett, Melinda Marshall, and Laura Sherbin said, "New research provides compelling evidence that diversity unlocks innovation and drives market growth."[4] The article describes two types of diversity, inherent and acquired. "Inherent Diversity involves traits you are born with, such as gender, ethnicity, and sexual orientation. Acquired Diversity involves traits you gain from experience: Working in another country can help you appreciate cultural differences."

The authors also suggest that diversity plays a crucial role in uncovering opportunities for innovation when the environment is optimal. "Diversity unlocks innovation by creating an environment where 'outside the box' ideas are heard. When minorities form a critical mass and leaders value differences, all employees can find senior people to go to bat for compelling ideas and can persuade those in charge of budgets to deploy resources to develop those ideas."[5]

The article cites some relevant statistics about what happens when diversity exists without inclusion. In addition, without an ambassador to support minority groups, their ideas and voices are usually not heard.

> Women are 20% less likely than straight white men to win endorsement for their ideas; people of color are 24% less likely; and LGBTs are 21% less likely. This costs their companies crucial market opportunities because numbers inherently diverse contributors understand the unmet needs in under-leveraged markets. We've found that when at least one member of a team has traits in common with the end-user, the entire team better understands that user. A team with a member who shares a client's ethnicity is 152% likelier than another team to understand that client.[6]

These numbers are not surprising for those who are the minority but sobering for those who are in power positions.

The article provides several solutions to the diversity and inclusion issues that minorities face on a daily basis in companies. Hewlett et al. suggest that it's important to give team members decision-making authority, share credit for success, provide actionable feedback, and solicit feedback from the team.[7] Through authentic, empathetic, and assertive leadership, these solutions can meet the needs of minorities, the majority, and the company's clients.

EQUITY

Equity is the most complex component of IDEA. The definition of equity is to give fair and equal opportunities and resources to employees based on their needs so they can succeed in their job, position, or career. Providing employees with equity may include but is not limited to training, coaching, special needs computers, interpreters, and even access to pertinent information for better decision making. Two examples of equity come to mind.

In this first example, my undiagnosed learning disability was initially an issue when I decided to go back to school. It was incredibly frustrating to keep pace with the work and my college peers because of the amount of weekly reading required.

I mention that I was undiagnosed because I did not receive information about the disability, nor did I know about my rights or the support available to help me through life until I was diagnosed in my thirties. That said, I graduated high school with a 1.7 grade-point average. After my diagnosis and receiving the support required, I earned my bachelor's degree in organizational management with a 3.8 grade-point average—a stark difference in performance.

In the second example, I encountered great difficulties learning new material when I became a national trainer. I struggled so much that my manager was not sure whether he could continue to keep me; the company then placed me on a performance improvement plan. To the company's credit, they gave me a coach who knew how to work with dyslexia. In less than a year, I had exceeded company evaluation scores. In both cases, equity was the factor that helped me succeed in my career. Absent equity, you would not be reading this book.

Equity is challenging because it requires companies and leaders to assign power equally across employees. For many in workplace power positions, equity is the last frontier to explore in the world of IDEA.

The conversation about equity seems to create the most discomfort and vulnerability for the majority and those in power. Providing equity to those who are not in control weakens the workplace dichotomy because it gives minorities authority over their careers and the ability to make decisions that help them reach their goals. It's a hurdle, especially when those in power have blind spots and, thus, a lack of empathy.

"Becoming Powerful Makes You Less Empathetic," a 2012 *Harvard Business Review* article by Lou Solomon, states that the more power you have, the less empathy you have.[8]

> Dacher Keltner, an author and social psychologist at University of California, Berkeley, has conducted empirical studies showing that people who have power suffer deficits in empathy, the ability to read emotions, and the ability to adapt behaviors to other people. In fact, power can actually change how the brain functions, according to research from Sukhvinder Obhi, a neuroscientist at Wilfrid Laurier University in Ontario, Canada.[9]

In addition, Elizabeth A. Segal, PhD, makes some excellent points in her *Psychology Today* article "Power Blocks Empathy." Segal found research that "confirms that people in power have lower levels of empathy compared to those who lack power. Those in power are simply not that interested in those below them. They view themselves as different and above others."[10]

Power is not all bad. It is necessary to get things done, Segal insists. "The challenge is to develop both the skills of power and the skills of empathy—and to know when to use each and when not to."[11] Dr. Segal also found that power plays a critical role in innovation and moving things forward. "Power can also encourage innovation. Feeling powerful frees us from feeling inhibited by what others think, so we are more willing to try different things, go against the grain, even push boundaries."[12] Both power and empathy are important to the conversation about equity. Those in power must be willing to share it for equity to exist. Without shared power, employees will not be able to request the necessary resources to level the workplace playing field.

ACCESSIBILITY

Accessibility means providing equitable access and intentionally removing barriers for those who are impaired. For example, if an employee uses a wheelchair, he would have uninhibited access to the workspace, bathroom, cafeteria, and other areas that help facilitate success in his job. Providing accessibility to employees can make a world of difference in their engagement, job performance, and morale.

Many years ago, when I was a manager for a nonprofit organization in Washington, D.C., I was responsible for overseeing my department's day-to-day operations and managing a couple of staff members. One staff member, Eddie, used a wheelchair. I thought this was odd because the tactical job description required frequent mobility. Some days we had to walk up and down steps and get in and out of the car, sometimes several times within an hour. Eddie had no problem doing the extra work to get in and out of his wheelchair when needed. He would climb the steps with his hands and maneuver his body into the car without asking for help. I remember telling Eddie that if he ever needed help to just ask. But he took offense at my offer. Later, I found out that he had worked for the organization for a while. However, his self-confidence was low, and although he didn't complain or ask for help, he needed it, yet he resented having to ask other workers to help him. At the time, it was hard to empathize with his circumstances because I didn't know anyone else who had a physical disability.

Eddie had a positive, upbeat personality. I was inspired, considering his circumstances. After working with Eddie for a few weeks, his cheerful, upbeat attitude waned. I soon learned that he was masking his true feelings. Underneath the smiles, Eddie was unhappy with his job because he didn't have the proper equipment and services to do it properly. Eddie felt that the organization would fire him if he complained because it didn't have the funds to provide the equipment and services he needed to perform well. He was also afraid that people would judge him for asking for help. Unfortunately, this issue revolved around social class and lack of education, but it is telling of the fears that class migrants experience when seeking help with resources.

Eventually, Eddie received a well-paid federal government job, which provided the accommodations necessary to do his job. In addition, he learned that by law, he could have requested the equipment and services he needed. Because he didn't know this, Eddie worked in fear for several years and maintained a job where he was unhappy, underpaid, and received unwarranted criticism for his performance. Due to fear and being uninformed, Eddie, like many employees who need access to resources, decided to keep his challenges to himself. Although Eddie's story had a happy ending, not all are so lucky.

Accessibility does not always mean disability. A variety of work situations require accessibility, such as for remote workers.

A couple of years ago, an engineering firm hired me to help remote employees access their internal servers. When I attended the first meeting with the president and senior leadership, I realized they didn't just need help with giving employees access to the servers; they needed help understanding why remote employees needed to be remote. The company president, who hired my company, was roadblocking the remote employee initiative, which slowed IT from solving the problem. The CEO of the company felt forced to allow employees to work remotely. When I had an opportunity to ask the CEO how he started the business, I could tell immediately that he was operating from an outdated paradigm. He was biased against remote employees, which influenced his senior leaders. The consensus among senior leadership boiled down to a trust issue. They were unsure what employees were doing when working from home without supervision. Later, one leader admitted that he worked from home and oddly also mentioned that research shows that employees who work at home are more productive.

The CEO's lack of empathy and buy-in for remote accessibility confused leadership. Because employees were told to work from home but knew they had no support, they worked ten- to sixteen-hour days to prove their worth and productivity. However, this backfired on the company because, over time, employees became less productive. For accessibility to be a part of the workplace culture, everyone must understand its importance, and leadership must be able to empathize with those who need accessibility.

SEVEN KEY IDEA RECOMMENDATIONS

1. Learn How to Have Candid Cross-Racial Conversations

Throughout my eighteen years of working with corporate leaders, cross-racial conversations emerge as the number one challenge to organizational initiatives. Glenn E. Singleton's 2015 book, *Courageous Conversations About Race: A Field Guide for Achieving Equity in Schools*, shares a framework about how to have challenging race conversations.

Singleton has the right idea. Multicultural education starts in a classroom, but it also requires ongoing multicultural discussions. That is, his book provides instructional reform, helping to bridge the gap for schools and districts; however, the conversation should extend beyond race and encompass the long-standing challenges that corporations, companies, and communities face in their inclusion, diversity, equity, and accessibility initiatives.

It's difficult for people from different cultures, ethnicities, and races to engage in courageous conversations because it can feel intimidating. Whether Black, white, red, brown, purple, or yellow, sometimes people feel threatened, accused, or even personally responsible for the wrongdoings that individuals of their race have done to another race. Although this is irrational, no one wants to be misjudged or associated with racism, crimes, or prejudice.

Leaders and employees are often hesitant. They fear rocking the boat because office norms pressure people into remaining politically correct. Multicultural conversations require finesse; world wars have started over less.

Leadership programs have attempted to break down barriers, but a few leadership training courses barely scratch the surface of multicultural and race nuances and the communication dynamics within an organization.

There are no magic bullets. You can see how the mere mention of this common phrase can turn minds to controversial topics between Black and white people. The word bullet can elicit thoughts of gang wars or police brutality, making the most competent communicator and listener uncomfortable or stumble for words. Most leadership seminars and sensitivity training workshops fail to teach, talk about, or practice multicultural communication skills beyond body language—and some neglect it altogether.

I've found leaders and employees tiptoeing around each other instead of learning how to communicate effectively; miscommunication and noncommunication divide corporations, teams, and communities on a national scale.

More often than not, when a company asks me to coach leaders on diversity or equity challenges, they look away and become fidgety once the discussion turns to race and gender equality. It could be that they feel insecure, accused, are having an inner dialogue, or just thinking. However, it's usually not the case that they do not want to have the conversation; they just don't know how.

Multicultural or racial conversations require emotional intelligence (EQ) and social intelligence (SQ). When leaders engage in difficult conversations, their ability to regulate their emotions is critical to leaning into the conversation instead of leaning away. Organizations need to be intentional about EQ because leaders need to be aware of their feelings and the feelings of others. Equally, they need to be intentional about SQ so leaders can communicate and have day-to-day interactions with employees, coworkers, customers, partners, and other stakeholders that support inclusion, diversity, equity, and access.

2. Conduct an Assessment

Imagine going to the doctor's office for a routine checkup, and your doctor fails to order labs and merely writes you a prescription without knowing what is wrong. Companies do this when they spend millions of dollars purchasing generic training and sending their leaders to three-day diversity workshops. Studies show that diversity training alone is not as impactful as a holistic approach, and "the skills and information that people get from a diversity training are forgotten quickly."[13] Interactive training, ongoing coaching, auditing, self-managed teams, and modernizing human resource processes and internal marketing produce a greater return.

> "Diversity training, in general, doesn't change much for any corporation."[14] And homogenous decision-making is one of the most significant barriers to solving real problems. Companies have greater success when they develop a diversity, inclusion and equity (DEI) task force, committee or council. However, companies cannot simply assemble diverse groups of people to solve their workplace culture diversity challenges; they must also follow up with individualized plans.

If you want to go fast, go alone; if you want to go far, go together.
—African proverb

3.   Assess the Hiring Process

One of the costliest challenges that organizations face is bias in their hiring process. From 2018 to 2020, many organizations have reached out to me to inquire about hiring more minorities and women.

Sometimes the answers are right in front of us, but we over-look them. For example, while working as a consultant for a construction management company, the vice president of human resources told me he had problems hiring, keeping, and develop-ing women and people of color. I asked him if he knew why. He said not really, because they were doubling down on their efforts for recruiting. I asked, "What does doubling down mean?" He said, "Well, we've devoted more marketing to the colleges that we recruit from."[15] He mentioned three top engineering colleges. I then asked him the names of other places from which they recruit. "What do you mean where else? I just told you these are the three schools that we recruit from," he said.[16] I asked, "Why just these three schools?" He said, "Because they're the best engineer schools in the nation, and most of our leaders have attended those schools. It makes it easy because we can get the best students from those schools."

The next day I delivered a training workshop to the executive leadership team. When the training session came to a close, I asked how many had attended one of the three colleges. Eighty percent of the executive leadership team raised their hands. After further investigation, I made another interesting discovery. Most of the minority talent they hired only stayed in the company eighteen months. However, although they hired minorities and women, most resigned, and many walked across the street to the competition. So, the company had no talent pool from which to promote when it came to succession planning. Like other organizations, their lead-ership was primarily fifty-year-old white males with very similar education and backgrounds.

Although it was not deliberate, neither was their hiring process. To hire more diverse individuals in your organization, leadership must understand where the bias lies. The construction engineer-ing company was no different than a lot of my clients. They were

subconsciously excluding women and people of color because of
their preferences and biases.

I also asked the vice president if he had ever thought about
recruiting from historically black colleges and universities (HBCUs),
or engineers in associations for minorities such as the National
Society of Black Engineers (NBSE) or American Indian Science and
Engineering Society (AISES)? He said, "Not really, because I really
don't know anyone there."[17] Again, I hear this story all the time from
my clients.

MINORITY RECRUITING, HIRING,
AND CAREER TRACK PLANS

- Recruiting from the same universities can cause a lack of diversity. When I was younger, an old fisherman told me that you
  must go where the rockfish are if you want to catch rockfish.
  So, if companies want to bring minorities on board, they must
  go where the minorities are. Today, it's seldom a matter of a
  pipeline problem; it's a matter of looking for the pipeline itself.
  Outside of searching for candidates at HBCUs, NBSE, or AISES,
  companies can recruit underrepresented minority professionals
  by posting or searching online for diversity job boards such as
  Jopwell, 2050, Women Who Code, Project Basta, Out and Equal,
  and many others.[18]
- When hiring minorities, companies must consider their pre-
  paredness to be inclusive. Class migrants are more motivated
  when they see leaders who look like they do because they can
  imagine themselves in that position. In other words, having
  diverse leaders or managers who are representative of staff
  shows a way forward because it signifies to minority employees that they can move up in the company. Doing so also offers
  minorities someone who understands the business and someone they can speak with who also understands their cultural
  challenges.
- Companies must analyze their talent management system and
  create a specialized career track for minorities that supports
  their unique needs and challenges. Its design should offer mentorship, exposure and stretch opportunities, access to resources,

and a map of how to excel in the organization. The map or path is not meant to be effortless, but it should be recognizable.

Overhauling a hiring practice is no easy feat, especially when an organization has operated the same way for thirty years. I recommend hiring an outside consultant or bringing in diversity, equity, and inclusion specialists such as a chief diversity officer or someone at a lower level specializing in diversity. Organizing a diverse hiring committee or recruitment agency is highly beneficial when hiring across different demographics, but leadership must be prepared to support the recommendations.

4. Measure Diversity and Inclusion Practices

Companies measure revenue, employee performance, and even how long bathroom supplies last. So why wouldn't they measure diversity and inclusion efforts? After all, what gets measured gets done. Peter Drucker is known for a similar adage: "what gets measured gets managed."[19] The moral of the story is that we pay more attention to the things we measure. Measurement provides data, and when we have metrics, we can analyze them and make process and system improvements.

My client calls usually begin with two questions: "What have you done so far as it pertains to diversity equity and inclusion? Have you measured the impact?" Most clients can answer the first question but not the second. At times, corporate leaders cannot answer either one because DE&I has not been clearly defined but remains an abstract and highly political concept. For years, companies have checked the box in this area with little thought and have not measured impact unless mandated. Worse, many companies don't maximize their survey results and hire minorities in only a few token positions—namely, as a chief diversity officer—but then fail to support the recommendations.

Companies that wish to remain competitive should develop an operations plan for diversity inclusion and equity initiative. The plan should identify specific and tangible goals that can be measured and accomplished within eighteen to twenty-four months. At Ascension Worldwide, we use the Global Diversity and Inclusion Benchmark to determine the starting point for organizations on their path toward becoming more diverse, equitable, and inclusive. Using this benchmark, we develop realistic short- and long-term goals that help organizations reach their DE&I objectives.

One of the most potent questions a company can ask itself is: If I could travel into the future and read an article about my company's diversity, inclusion, and equity success, what would the headline be? And how would the major points of the article read? From here, we work backward and reverse engineer the goal setting, which helps the company achieve this imagined future.

5. Incorporate Inclusion into Performance Evaluations

When companies are serious about creating an inclusive culture, they integrate it into their leaders' performance evaluations. Dr. Lynn Scott, a former mentor, once told me, "If you want people to be more inclusive, tie it to their compensation plan and promotion evaluation. Then they will become more inclusive."[20] I will add to his comment. Hire more inclusive leaders; that way, hiring and developing inclusivity for class migrants and minorities becomes natural—something leaders just do.

Now that we understand that inclusion means "getting asked to dance," we need to ask how organizations can measure inclusivity? That requires another chapter, but many tools are available that allow companies to benchmark IDEA and gain insights that help them develop and foster an inclusive culture.

Although inclusion is a qualitative metric, it can be measured in a fashion similar to measuring employee satisfaction and engagement. In addition, Employee Resource Groups (ERGs) or Business Resource Groups (BRGs) are valuable resources that can aid in both D&I discovery and strategy; the fact that an organization has ERGs speaks volumes. Those who participate in ERGs or BRGs are good indicators of where gaps may exist in terms of inclusivity. Organizations create opportunities for immersive learning when they encourage managers to volunteer their time to support ERGs and BRGs.

Paolo Gaudiano, chief scientist at Aleria, said, "An effective way to measure inclusion in your organization is to create a questionnaire with a list of 'incidents of exclusion,' and ask people in your firm to indicate whether and how often they experience these types of exclusion."[21] To obtain the best results, companies must ensure that all respondents can complete surveys and questionnaires anonymously.

6. Develop Formal Mentoring Programs

The COVID-19 pandemic in 2020 and 2021 has challenged diversity, inclusion, and equity efforts to the nth degree. As organizations open their doors again, they must work even harder to ensure that employees feel included and feel a sense of distributed justice. Distributed justice, in a word, means equity. It refers to social justice, which is "the balancing of individuals' claims to all of the possible benefits of social cooperation."[22] Statistics show that the balance of fairness continues to be lopsided.

> Black and Hispanic workers continue to be underrepresented in the STEM workforce. Blacks make up 11% of the U.S. workforce overall but represent 9% of STEM workers, while Hispanics comprise 16% of the U.S. workforce but only 7% of all STEM workers . . . STEM jobs have relatively high earnings compared with many non-STEM jobs, and the earnings gap persists even after controlling for educational attainment.[23]

Although underrepresentation is primarily a matter of the candidate selection process, class migrants and minorities are apt to sense distributed justice when they have equal representation and access to the same benefits as their white counterparts.

Class migrants who manage to get into a professional position typically flounder in their current role because they have little to no support transitioning from college to the workplace. In addition, they are excluded from the organic or informal mentoring that most white male employees have. Notably, minorities face a different set of challenges than white employees.

Many white and minority participants in my unconscious bias training courses said that mentoring was instrumental to their career success. It helped them learn the business, navigate office politics, gain access to high visibility meetings and projects, learn negotiation skills, and connect with people of influence.

A study sponsored by JPMorgan Chase found "strong evidence that mentors can help young people build their identities as workers, help them apply their school learning to work, teach them soft skills that can be essential to career success, improve their attitudes and motivations about work, and generally give young workers opportunities to learn new skills and how to be part of a team. This sets the stage for ongoing career success and tangible rewards, such as higher compensation, advancement up career ladders, and greater job stability."[24]

Mentorships have transformed my personal and professional life. I feel so strongly about it that I've dedicated a whole chapter in this book to mentoring. However, developing a successful mentoring program is labor-intensive work, even for companies that are D&I savvy.

7. Develop an Internship Program

Internships are one of the most impactful ways to increase diversity, inclusion, and equity mutually beneficial to the intern and the company. Internships are valuable career experiences for future employees, especially minorities and class migrants. Interns are a source of low-cost talent for short stints. They truly are a win-win.

At Ascension Worldwide, we have hired interns from Towson University, Kentucky University, Saint Bonaventure University, and Johns Hopkins University. Most of these universities have a moderately diverse talent pool.

Before their start at Ascension, most interns have no social media presence. Three months later, they have a client persona, a social media marketing plan and accounts on Twitter, Instagram, Facebook, LinkedIn, and YouTube. Amber Royal, a graduate of Johns Hopkins University, said our internship program was the sole reason she landed a six-figure job at a nearby medical center. She gained valuable work experience by working on analytics for customer personas and helped our team with high-level marketing strategies. We also integrate a mentoring and professional development component into our internship program, which we recommend to our clients and help them implement.

7

The Power of Belonging

Belonging is being part of something bigger than yourself. But it's also the courage to stand alone and to belong to yourself above all else.—Dr. Brené Brown

Envision sitting in a meeting as a new employee in your first real job. Several high-caliber, influential leaders are in the room. You are nervous because it is your first day and you do not know much about your job. The people around the table know all the rules of engagement. Although you have some experience in this industry and consider yourself an out-of-the-box thinker, you are not quite sure how others will perceive or value your ideas. The vice president of your department shares an industry challenge the company is experiencing. You are familiar with this challenge because you have studied it for the past two years but only in theory. Then the vice president asks, "Who has a solution?" No one speaks up. You know the answer, but you can't seem to get your hand up or mouth open. It seems like ten minutes have passed, yet it has only been three seconds. Your palms are sweating, and you can feel your heartbeat in your head; you feel like you are about to have an anxiety attack. You know the answer, but you are not sure if you belong to the group; therefore, you do not know how they will respond. Because this is your first significant interaction, you do not want to step on toes, come off as a know-it-all, or submit an idea that others can poke holes in or shoot down. So instead of sharing your vision, you slump back into your seat, keep your mouth shut, and wait for someone else to speak up. Whether in our personal or professional lives, we all have experienced this scenario in some form or fashion.

MASLOW'S HIERARCHY OF NEEDS

Maslow's hierarchy of needs is a theory Abraham Maslow proposed in a1943 paper, *A Theory of Human Motivation*. Maslow argues that individuals must "satisfy lower level basic needs before progressing on to meet higher level growth needs."[1] His hierarchy begins with our basic needs or *physiological* needs (air, water, shelter, sleep), then the need for *safety and security* (personal, financial, and health). After meeting those needs, Maslow says our needs shift to *love and belonging* (friendship, intimacy, family, and connection), then to the need for *self-esteem* (respect, status, recognition). Finally, once all other needs are met, we reach the need for *self-actualization* (achievement of personal goals and reaching our full potential).

Howard Ross, the author of *Our Search for Belonging: How Our Need to Connect Is Tearing Us Apart*, says that Maslow was wrong. The primary motivator is the need to belong. Physiological needs for safety and security come next.

Like the earlier scenario of the first day at work, have you ever had a great idea, but you held back because you weren't sure if you belonged? Have you or someone you know ever endured physical or emotional pain, or financial hardship, to experience belonging? If you know anyone who has been part of a sorority or fraternity before college campuses outlawed hazing, then you have seen how the need to belong motivates us.

The military is another example. People lay down their lives not just for their country but for their families and buddies who fight next to them on the battlefield. In World War II, Japanese kamikaze pilots trained to be human bombs. The pilots, locked into the planes with no landing gear or weapons other than the explosive in the plane's nose, fought to their death. These pilots had no regard for personal safety or physical needs. They put themselves in harm's way for one reason: honor—to belong to something bigger than themselves. And in the Japanese culture, no accomplishment is more extraordinary than the sense of belonging that honor brings to you, your family, and your country. Young kamikaze pilots trained to put their lives on the line, not for their honor but the honor of their families. This ideology supports Howard's argument that belonging is not only a potent need but a primary need that supersedes even physical safety.

THE DETRIMENTS OF NOT BELONGING

Research shows that when someone first turns to drugs or crime, they are usually trying to fit in or cope with emotional pain and feelings of rejection and alienation brought on by a lack of parental involvement, a dysfunctional family, or weak social relationships. In addition, "students are at higher risk for dropping out, joining gangs, or using drugs."[2]

> Most children fail in school not because they lack the necessary cognitive skills, but because they feel detached, alienated, and isolated from others and from the educational process. When children feel rejected by others, they either internalize the rejection and learn to hate themselves or externalize the rejection and learn to hate others. In *East of Eden* (1952), John Steinbeck described it as the story of the human soul:[3]
>
> "The greatest terror a child can have is that he is not loved, and rejection is the hell of fears. I think everyone in the world to a large or small extent has felt rejection. And with rejection comes anger, and with anger some kind of crime in revenge for the rejection, and with crime, guilt—and there is the story of mankind."[4] Even Maslow "believed that most maladjustment and emotional illness in our society could be traced to the failure to gratify the basic human need for belonging."[5]

Whether it's political, sports teams, religion, company culture, family culture, or social class, people will do just about anything to feel a sense of belonging.

THE DEEP DESIRE TO BELONG

When we are born, we have an inherent connection to our mother. Although we cannot form words yet, we know to whom we belong by sight, smell, and voice. As we gain more experience in life, belonging becomes ambiguous. But, social rules and group-based hierarchies decide who will be allowed into the clique or in-group—this is where class and bias come into the picture.

An article written by the Royal Society reinforces the need for connection in the earliest stage of our lives:

> Early in development, children seek to affiliate with others and to form long-lasting bonds with their group members. Furthermore, when children are deprived of a sense of belonging, it has negative consequences for their well-being ... Humans are deeply dependent on their group members. Only through copying their skills and practices are we able to learn how to survive in diverse, and sometimes even hostile environments [1,2]. Only through cooperating with them are we able to gain access to food, shelter, and protection from attack [3]. Children are born into these social groups. From early in development, they interact not only with their caregivers, but with their peers and other adults [4].[6]

WHY IS BELONGING SO IMPORTANT?

Belonging drives everything we do. I remember my freshman year at Oxon Hill High School like it was yesterday. As a freshman, I entered a new world comprised of students who had attended different middle schools. When I say students, I mean girls I did not yet know. To be liked by girls is one of the most potent desires a young man can have. At least that was my story then. I quickly assessed the different ways I could access a feeling of belonging there. I could join a sports team. I could get good grades. I could sell drugs. I could be the best dressed, or maybe I could be the class clown. None of these strategies seemed to work for my personality and my level of development. So, I became an outsider, a person who felt no connection to any particular group. I was not a jock, a scholar, a cool kid, or a jokester. I was the kid whose parents didn't quite make enough money to have the same luxuries as my school peers. To make up for the gap in household finances, I worked.

At the end of my freshman year, I noticed Nathaniel, an upperclassman who seemed to know just about everyone in school. He was in with the cool kids, the jocks, the kids who sold drugs, and he seemed always to have the latest tennis shoes. I could not articulate it back then, but I knew this kid had a sense of belonging. He was not in any of the groups, yet he belonged to all of them. I had to find out his secret. One day between classes, I saw him talking to my sister, Selina. After class, I had a conversation with her.

Me: How do you know Nathaniel?

Selina: He has a class with me.

Me: How does he know everyone?

Selina: Because he works at the mall for the sporting goods company, you know the one that sells the sweatshirts everyone loves?

Right then and there, I made a plan. The next day after school, I went to the sporting goods store find out what made him so cool and why everyone liked him. I walked in and saw him working with the customer. I pretended to browse. After he noticed me, our conversation went like this: ere's how it went.

Nathaniel: Hey man, can I help you?

Me: Yes, you can; I was wondering how you know everyone in high school and had relationships with all these different people and groups.

Nathaniel: Are you doing some type of project or something?

Me (realizing that I probably sounded like a stalker): Yes.

Nathaniel: Oh, that's easy. All the kids go school shopping or come here to get the latest pair of sneakers. So everyone knows me, plus I give the cute girls and the football team a discount.

Me: That's it?

Nathaniel: Yup! That's it.[7]

After being shocked at how simple it was to solve this mystery, I realized that I knew the secret ingredient to be liked by all. And it didn't require me to try out for the football team. At the time, this was perfect because I was already used to working. I had just one small problem. It seemed that every student who was interested in working wanted to work at the sporting goods store. The manager told me he received thirty applications a week from kids just like me. I conjured up another plan that would land me this golden opportunity before summer started and more people began applying. I applied for the job twice a week until the hiring manager knew me by my first name.

No matter how many times I brought in my application, they somehow could not find it on file. After a few weeks, the hiring manager remembered my name and knew I was persistent. Finally, within two months, there was an opening. I bumped into two hiring managers flipping through a stack of résumés. When they looked up, they saw me standing there with a big smile on my face. The hiring manager threw me an employee T-shirt and said, "We'll see you this Saturday." I had finally landed the job of my dreams based on sheer persistence. This type of determination was advantageous in pursuing future goals.

It wasn't easy to believe, but one job changed everything. Once my classmates learned that I worked at the sporting goods store, I went from invisible to popular. My peers would walk up to me and say something like, "Hey, I heard you're working at the sporting goods store. Do you know when the new Jordans are coming out?" Sometimes players from the football team would ask if we sold size 14 cleats. Even the cool kids approached me to inquire about the new colors of Champion sweatshirts—Champion T-shirts were "fly" in the '90s; students matched them with their Nike Air Force 1s. I went from being a pimply faced freshman to an authority on sporting goods and apparel. At the age of sixteen, I planned and executed an elaborate plan—all in the name of belonging.

Belonging is not always found so easily. However, most people have had similar experiences in their teenage years when you're impressionable and self-esteem teeters on your ability to fit in and belong. This phenomenon does not start or stop in high school. We strive to belong as young as four years old, and it becomes our modus operandi or particular method of doing something. That is, at the deepest level of our being, we are all motivated to belong, through family, sports, theater, music, business, book clubs, illegal methods, or physical aesthetics.

Whatever affects one directly, affects all indirectly. I can never be what I ought to be until you are what you ought to be. This is the interrelated structure of reality. —Martin Luther King Jr.

THE SIX BARRIERS TO BELONGING

Shame

In a 2020 *60 Minutes* interview, Brené Brown shared that shame is a universal emotion that everyone experiences. She says shame is a focus on self, whereas guilt focuses on behavior. For example, shame: "I am bad"; guilt: "I did something bad."

Renee says that we are more likely to respond with empathy and make changes when we focus on behavior. I will add, shame leads to covering. Covering leads to psychological erosion. I will talk more about both of these concepts in the next section.

For some of us, it's easier to understand shame by thinking about past experiences. Here are a couple of scenarios that might jog your memory about your own experiences with shame.

- Have you ever made a major mistake at work, and your boss attacked your character instead of focusing on your actions and discussing how you can change them?
- Have you ever received a poor grade in school, and your teacher or parent comments on your smarts?
- Have you ever made a mistake in front of a group, and your spouse/partner belittles you?
- Have you ever misunderstood your child, and he attacks your parenting skills?

If you have experienced any of these situations, you know what it is like to experience shame. Shame does not feel good. It demoralizes you. When children and adults feel shame, they are more likely to underperform, make mistakes, become defensive, withdraw, emotionally disconnect, and become more prone to illness and biases.

Some fifteen years ago, I worked for an engineering design subsidiary of General Electric as a mechanical designer. I worked closely with the senior engineers and drafters to lay out mechanical drawings for office buildings. Fred Smith, the gentleman who ran our department, was a hard worker but seemed to lack emotional and social intelligence. Fred had worked for the company for nine years and he had not advanced as far as he had hoped. On top of that, he had a dysfunctional relationship with his family. At times it would spill into his work life. One day Fred and I were working on a project with a tight deadline. Fred asked me to start a layout on a mechanical drawing. I understood the criticality of the project, so I skipped lunch to complete the drawing.

When I handed the drawing to Fred, he yelled and cussed, asking me if I was stupid or unable to follow directions. He believed the drawing font/text size was incorrect. We had a standard text size for each project; as a designer, I was supposed to know the text size from memory. After Fred's verbal attack, I had a physiologic response. My nose started bleeding, and I felt angry and scared all at the same time. I was angry because I felt attacked and in the wrong. I was scared because Fred had threatened the jobs of other employees. I was also new to the team and still learning, so I was unsure of my skills and felt a little ashamed. After I checked the font size, I gave the drawing back to Fred and told him it was correct. He still challenged me, but after he inspected it himself, he apologized. Unfortunately, the damage was done.

After the incident, we lacked trust and communication between us, and my performance plummeted. In this situation and many others, Fred would attack the character of his team members instead of coaching them on behavior changes. My experience was mild compared to that of Tony, a senior designer on our team.

Tony, middle-aged, was not in the best shape. It didn't help that he loved to eat doughnuts daily. He was an exceptionally talented designer, but he would miss things from time to time, just like everyone does. Tony was constantly under verbal attack from Fred. After every heated meeting, Tony would head downstairs to the coffee shop for a couple of doughnuts and a soda. After I returned from a vacation, I noticed that Tony wasn't at his desk. We were pretty close. Every Monday, we would talk about family or catch up on what we did over the weekend. As it turned out, Tony was in the hospital; he had undergone triple bypass heart surgery.

Along with the doughnuts, the pressure and stress at work had caught up with him. Tony not only was overweight, but also led a sedentary lifestyle. Although he showed up early at work to start his projects, he was physically and emotionally burned out each day. In turn, Tony made more mistakes, which made Fred furious. Tony recovered, but he was never the same. He consistently second-guessed his work and always mumbled about how much he hated Fred. Tony's work performance got worse and worse.

The story about Tony, Fred, and me may sound extreme, but ones similar are common in the workplace. As a leadership trainer and diversity and inclusion consultant, I could write a book about similar stories I've heard from employees across the country. I want to be clear about this story: Fred is not 100 percent the villain, and Tony and I are not 100 percent the victims. When someone such as Fred shames his employees to that degree and people such as Tony and I allow it, it means that each of us has had our fair share of shame in our lifetimes. The difference is in how that shows up in our behavior later. What we experience in our adult lives mirrors our experiences in our formative years. This action is not about blaming anyone; it's about being aware of where shame comes from and how it emotionally and physically manifests and interferes with leading others and living a productive, healthy life.

> Shame is the warm feeling that washes over us, making us feel small, flawed and never good enough. — Brené Brown[8]

Covering

The feeling of thinking we are bad or not good enough leads to covering. Kenji Yoshino, a gay Asian American man and author of the book *Covering: The Hidden Assault on Our Civil Rights*, says everybody covers.

> To cover is to downplay a disfavored trait so as to blend into the mainstream. Because all of us possess stigmatized attributes, we all encounter pressure to cover in our daily lives. Racial minorities are pressed to "act white" by changing their names, languages, or cultural practices. Women are told to "play like men" at work. Gays are asked not to engage in public displays of same-sex affection. The devout are instructed to minimize expressions of faith, and individuals with disabilities are urged to conceal the paraphernalia that permit them to function.[9]

Covering is also an unconscious/subconscious strategy class migrants and outsiders (minorities) use to fit into social norms within the workplace environment and personal social settings.

As a trainer and consultant, I have heard many experiences of people from all walks of life covering one identity or another. Josephine, a woman engineer at a large engineering firm in Des Moines, Iowa, told me she changes her name to Joe on her résumé to get a job in her field because it's male dominated. Haruto, a Japanese manager at a large automotive company in Michigan, changed his name to Harry because he wanted to feel included as his peers would not attempt to say his name for fear of mispronunciation. Brandon, a Black human resource professional at a tech company in Irvine, California, shared that he changes his voice for fear of intimidating his white colleagues. Helen, a Caribbean-born social worker, spends hours each day disguising her accent so her clients won't know she's an immigrant, which allows her to develop trust with her counterparts and clients. Andrea, a project manager for an international consulting firm, does not attend company functions because her partner is a woman, but everyone assumes otherwise.

People with disabilities are highly skilled at covering. As an adult dyslexic, I employed many strategies to cover my disability. Some included not self-advocating or asking for help on assignments that involved extra reading and data organization. In addition, although it strengthened my ability to be independent, I would not clarify directions for fear of coming off as incompetent or unsure of myself.

When people with disabilities cover, the side effects can manifest in multiple ways. When the workload becomes too great to handle, some become frustrated, overwhelmed, defensive, or withdraw altogether.

For whatever reason people cover, the by-product is psychological erosion. Psychological erosion happens when people must consistently cover their identities. The act itself disconnects a person's identity, causing him to feel loss, cognitive dissonance, and negative bias.

Psychological erosion lowers self-esteem and confidence, which affects work performance and intimacy. Both personal and professional relationships require intimacy (also called closeness) because it allows each person to connect to the other authentically. Without an authentic connection, one or both people feel a sense of coercion and a great deal of emotional discomfort. In turn, this feeling leads to a disconnect from others and a disconnect from self. It's not about growing into a better person; it's about hiding an identity that could be a significant strength or asset to building relationships through empathy and authenticity.

When psychological erosion materializes, people typically display a lack of efficacy and tend to retreat into themselves. For some people, it leads to overeating or excessive drug or alcohol use.

Erosion can also manifest as self-loathing, self-sabotaging, and self-censoring behaviors. It has even shown up as overachievement and is a trigger for physical and mental conditions. Most people have experienced covering to some degree, but they may not know that they're covering because they've been doing it for so long. This section does not aim to beat up anyone for covering but to bring about awareness. Later in this chapter, I'll share some tips on creating a culture of belonging where people feel safe enough to uncover.

A person who is constantly covering will develop shame of self that is irreparably damaging.

Lack of Inclusion

Inclusion and diversity discussions now include belonging. It is important to understand the difference between belonging and inclusion. Inclusion is when people offer or invite others into a space or conversation. Belonging is when that person feels comfortable in that space and feels like she belongs. Many companies, hiring managers, and communities confuse the two. Here is an example: The only woman at a male-dominated engineering firm is asked to sit in on an important project meeting. Although the woman is seated at the table, she may not feel comfortable giving advice or ideas if the environment is not favorable. Inclusion is the first step. We must bring people who are different into our spaces professionally and personally to gain their perspective. Once people feel included, the next step is to create a culture of belonging. When people feel like they belong, they share ideas and give feedback.

Here are some examples of how our blind spots, no matter how unintentional, can make others feel excluded: While working for the Department of Employment Services in downtown Washington, D.C., my colleagues and I frequented different restaurants. One day, as we were leaving the office for lunch, someone mentioned asking

Sarah, a newer employee, to join us. Without thinking, I said Sarah is a vegan and probably would not feel comfortable going to a place that served beef and chicken. Although this may have been true, and although my intentions were not to make Sarah feel excluded, I unintentionally excluded her by not inviting her. My intentions were good; the outcome was not. I persuaded my colleagues to exclude Sarah by not giving her the chance to decline the offer. When we returned, Sarah asked where we went for lunch. I told her that we had eaten at a Greek restaurant, but it only served beef, lamb, and chicken dishes. To my surprise, Sarah said she knew the place because it has delicious vegan dishes. At that time in my life, I was not familiar with diversity and inclusion concepts. Instead of apologizing to Sarah for not inviting her, I just changed the subject. Weeks after our lunch conversation, Sarah requested to be moved to a different team. Later, she told me she didn't feel comfortable with our team because we were not welcoming. What Sarah was really saying was that she felt like an outsider, and we were not inclusive.

Like my experience with Sarah, most people are not aware that they exclude others. Unfortunately, excluding others is sometimes easier than taking the risk of making a mistake. When we make mistakes, we feel uncomfortable and a little bit shameful. Bias kicks in, and subconsciously we prevent ourselves from being in that position again. Although we may want to invite Sarah to lunch, our brain is trying to protect us from feeling bad about poor decisions we've made in the past, so we unconsciously exclude her.

Whether it's inviting someone to lunch or a high-profile meeting, or new neighbors to a cookout, our brain is looking for sameness and comfort. If we are not aware of these blind spots, we can exclude others and miss opportunities to get to know people who differ from us. Inclusion requires effort as well as taking a bit of risk.

Lack of Experiences

Experiences or their lack create perspective. It's challenging to understand a person's point of view if you have never experienced what they have experienced, been in the same situation, or had the same circumstances as they did. In the world of diversity, inclusion, and equity, we call this perspective taking. Perspective taking allows a person to understand another person's vantage point, which is critical to creating a sense of belonging.

Stephen Covey, the author of *The 7 Habits of Highly Effective People*, hit the nail on the head when he quoted Theodore Roosevelt: "People don't care how much you know until they know how much you care."[10] When people know you care, they let down their guard and become open to receiving information. When you have experiences similar to others, this happens quickly. Habit 5 in Covey's book draws our attention to the importance of communication: "Seek first to understand, then to be understood."[11] More specifically, asking questions and actively listening can help us understand a person's experience. It's not always practical to gain the experiences of others, so the best way to understand what it's like to walk in someone else's shoes is to listen.

Perspective taking requires active listening (showing interest, concern, and creating a mutual understanding) and reflective listening (recognizing how the speaker feels and empathizing), which involves self-awareness, social intelligence, and emotional intelligence. Combined, this is considered interpersonal competence.

Misinterpretation occurs when we interrupt, judge, jump to conclusions, and focus on our reply to the speaker. Perspective taking requires us to be aware of and regulate our propensity to react. Active listening is a skill that leaders must hone if they want to influence people effectively and make them feel like they belong. It involves maintaining focus on what is being said, allowing the speaker to complete her thoughts and ideas, and taking the time to comprehend the message and its meaning by pausing to ask questions and paraphrasing before devising and delivering a response. When leaders fail to listen actively and fail to identify, understand, and empathize with the perspectives of others, employees suppress engagement and collaborative communication, which decreases creative thinking, participation, and team cohesiveness. Organizations that operate under authoritative leadership styles don't practice perspective taking, which produces a culture of bias, exclusion, inequity, distrust, demotivation, and further in-group–out-group division.

In the introduction, I mentioned that I delivered a keynote speech on class divide in the workplace and its implications at the 2019 SHRM Inclusion conference, a presentation about class bias and the challenges that class migrants face. Maria, one of the attendees, approached me after the presentation and asked me about the best way to get leaders to understand the difficulty employees have in communicating effectively in the workplace when English is not their first language.

She said the leaders in her company heard her. Yet, they still did not understand the gravity of the problem because they are not bilingual and have not worked in environments where English was not the predominant language. As Maria shared her frustrations, I listened, and I thought I understood what she meant about it being "difficult for employees." After an experience in South America, it was evident that I had not understood after all.

One month after speaking with Maria, I flew to Viña del Mar, Chile, where I delivered my first international presentation on inclusive leadership at the International Organizational Development Association. One evening after the conference, I went sightseeing with a couple of other presenters and participants. While walking around the streets, I realized that I had forgotten to eat that day. Everyone else had eaten at the conference, but I was too busy conversing with attendees to make sure my presentation went over well. I left the group and headed back to my Airbnb, about twenty minutes outside the city overlooking the shore. I thought I could just run down to a local restaurant to grab a bite to eat, but all of the restaurants were closed except one. I had been practicing my Spanish, but it was sketchy. I still only knew a couple of common phrases and polite greetings. Closer to the city, most of the people were bilingual. The further from town, the further we were from English-speaking residents. As soon as I walked into the restaurant, I said, "Hola!" After hello, it was all downhill. Although I could speak and understand a few Spanish words, I was hungry and tired—not ideal for active and reflective listening.

I was operating on what Daniel Kahneman calls the "fast brain," which is similar to the heuristics, mental short-cuts, and system-1 thinking discussed in chapter 4. In fast-brain mode, we have blind spots, biases, and knee-jerk reactions based on past experiences. In this case, I had little to no experience with language barriers. Once the waitress took my order and started speaking Spanish, my brain froze. The only words I could conjure up were yes and thank you, "Si" and "gracias,"respectively. I wanted to order a chicken sandwich, but the waitress thought I said chicken omelet. Why would I want a chicken omelet at 11 p.m.? I wouldn't and didn't, but that's what she served me because I was impatient, not paying attention, and frustrated with my inability to speak and comprehend Spanish. I ate the omelet anyway.

I can only imagine a day in the life of someone who isn't proficient in English and tries to navigate the U.S. corporate world. Most of the American workforce already has significant communication barriers—and they speak English! The language barrier essentially suffocated my voice. I felt isolated and excluded; once again, I was the outsider. I finally understood some of the frustrations that Maria, from the SHRM conference, experienced.

Like Maria and many others who face communication barriers, I settled for something I didn't want because it was easier than making a fuss and less painful than revealing my language inadequacies. We unconsciously learn to navigate "around people" and our environment to enjoy pleasure and prevent ourselves from experiencing pain or displeasure.

When I returned from Chile, I began my training workshops by sharing my language barrier challenges with different cultural groups. The bilingual participants' eyes widened, and they vigorously shook their heads in acknowledgment and agreement. Although many trainees struggled to speak because of their accents, they felt psychologically safe to do so. That is, they felt like they were in the in-group. They felt heard, understood, valued, and sensed that they belonged.

Several people were eager to share their experiences. One man from Korea asked if I could give special training to his nonbilingual managers to help them understand employee challenges. I was in awe that my story resonated with so many people. I realize it was not necessarily my storytelling skills, but instead, my experience that they found relatable. Because of this, they felt a strong connection. Cognitively trying to understand where a person is coming from is essential, but it does not make up for having the experience yourself. Does this mean we should seek out experiences to help us relate to others? Yes. But it depends on how vested you are in understanding the Marias of the world and creating a space for belonging.

Lack of Guidance

Nothing is more welcoming than arriving at a new place and being greeted at the front door. We connect better when someone shows us the ropes. Whether it's our first day at a new school, in a new neighborhood, or at a new job, we all need a guide to introduce us to our new environment. Those new to any social setting need direction because they are unaware of the unspoken social rules of engagement. They do not know the power dynamics. They do not know when to speak up at a meeting, what jokes are acceptable, what tables not to sit at during lunch, or who to ask for help. Guides help us navigate the unknown.

For a student, a guide might be the kid sitting next to him in school; in the workplace, a seasoned coworker in the department; at home, a neighbor who has kids attending the same school. No matter the situation, a guide can bring a sense of acceptance, belonging, and comfort. Guides can teach you the social norms and implicit or unspoken rules in your personal and professional life.

In 2019 my wife and I purchased a vacation house in San Juan, Puerto Rico. As mentioned, I did not speak much Spanish. We were new to the neighborhood, and we had a slew of communication barriers. Within two days, several neighbors stopped by to introduce themselves and ask if we needed anything. One neighbor, Julio, went the extra mile to make sure we felt comfortable. He helped us find everything we needed, including grocery stores, shopping malls, and home improvement stores. If we needed a ladder or water hose, Julio would walk across the street like he was reading our minds. He also helped us fix up the house and became our guide to everything San Juan. He even treated us to a ride on his fishing boat. Although we were a little nervous because the vessel was deteriorating and the motor kept stalling, we felt a sense of belonging.

Without a guide, people can feel intimidated, isolated, and unwelcome in a new environment. People who care help us straighten that learning curve. For instance, some neighborhoods have self-designated families who welcome and assist new neighbors. Schools often have a buddy system to help new kids become familiar with their environment. And some companies assign mentors who support new employees through the onboarding process.

When employees feel like they belong, it opens the door to an engaged, innovative, and synergistic culture. No matter your complexion, no one can thrive when excluded, sidelined, or left to their own devices. When companies foster belonging, employees gain acceptance, affinity, kinship, self-esteem, and confidence. Although we don't always know what drives us, we gain social identity, social value, status, empowerment, and access to resources that can help us perform better when we belong to a social group within an organization.

> Social identity is that part of an individual's self-concept which derives from his knowledge of his membership in a social group (or groups) together with the value and emotional significance attached with that membership ... It is not enough to belong to an organization, but a person needs to feel connected to the group.[12] —Henri Tajfel, social psychologist

Lack of Authenticity

Authenticity does not always lead to belonging, but it is a critical component to getting there. *The Dog Whisperer,* hosted by Cesar Millan, helps us understand the nuances of authenticity. In a 2004 series, Cesar helps dog owners develop better relationships with their animals. One woman said she could not get her dog to calm down and behave. He educated her by explaining that animals have a primal sense that allows them to see and feel energy. When you are scattered, Cesar would say, you put off energy that makes the dog discombobulated. Although the dog cannot communicate this with you, it inherently picks up on that vibe and reacts.

Each human has a primal sense, too. Both humans and animals get these feelings automatically. Call it a sixth sense or intuition; we are not aware of it because we're so busy in the minutiae of life and work. Humans and animals use this sense to detect whether a person is authentic. Dogs, for instance, growl or bark when they sense a threat. Humans can distinguish the sincerity of a smile with their eyes. If we perceive that a person is sincere, we trust him; if not, our fight, flight, or freeze mechanism kicks in, and our behaviors correspond.

Have you ever had a salesperson walk up to you in the store and dive straight into a pitch without asking about or understanding your needs? A salesperson who approaches you like this cannot be authentic because she doesn't know you. That is, like the salesperson, people cannot speak to your needs or understand your perspective if they never inquire to find out. Whether we're in a retail store, workplace, or a social setting, our brains can pick up signals that something's off. That's when skepticism and distrust set in. It's no different from the dogs Cesar works with on *The Dog Whisperer;*

when we sense something's amiss, we become apprehensive and on guard. It only takes a moment, a bad gut feeling, a roll of the eyes, or a hunch before we either run for the hills or zero in on other signals that demonstrate inauthenticity. When people are inauthentic, belonging isn't in the cards.

When we don't come across as authentic, walls go up, and trust goes down.

The best salespeople are authentic. I will never forget my first experience with Donna Hurley, a realtor who helped me purchase my first home. Until I met her, every realtor I worked with showed me homes outside my requirements. In their defense, I had a shoestring budget and needed more space than my money would allow. Instead of telling me that they could not help me achieve my goal, they showed me a bunch of houses that, in my opinion, were unsuitable. Some realtors said things such as, "This is the best you're going to find." Others tried to coerce me to put in an offer on houses that looked dilapidated. It was not until I meant Donna that I experienced an authentic realtor. Unlike the others, she asked me a lot of questions to try to understand my situation. She told me upfront that I would have to look at many houses to find one in my price range. She also assured me that she would work hard to find a suitable home for my family and me if I was willing to do the same. Something about her questions, patience, and energy made me trust her. In less than three months, she helped me find the perfect house that met all of my requirements in terms of neighborhood and community. Through authenticity, Donna and I developed a friendship and a business relationship and have had numerous business transactions over the years. I later sat on the board of her nonprofit organization for nearly a decade. When authenticity exists, people can see eye to eye, and they are open to ideas, alternatives, and working together.

CREATING A CULTURE OF BELONGING

Creating a culture of belonging starts with one person who—intentionally—takes the initiative to create a safe space for everyone, especially class migrants and minorities, who are usually in the outgroup. It also requires getting to know people, learning about their needs, goals, and challenges.

It makes no difference if you are the CEO of a Fortune 500 company headquartered in New York, a human resources manager of a medium-size nonprofit in the Midwest, a Canadian police officer patroling Vancouver, a soccer mom in the suburbs outside Washington, D.C., or a single parent living in Detroit, Michigan—everyone has the opportunity to create a culture of belonging within his sphere of influence. If each person steps up to create a safe space for someone else, it leaves a residual effect. Sometimes a simple hello can make a positive difference because the law of reciprocity encourages a hello back. Then the next person you encounter does the same. Eventually, you reach a tipping point, the culture becomes symbiotic, and the social norm to engage with one another is authentic and inclusive, where everyone feels that they belong. It only takes one person to start a chain reaction that can transform an entire culture. Every company or neighborhood has that person who cares about others, and everyone knows and feels it.

One of my first engineering jobs was at Summer Consultants, a mechanical, electrical, and plumbing consulting firm located in McLean, Virginia. Fran, the company president, took me to lunch my first day on the job. He made a genuine effort to get to know me personally, not just professionally. Fran was also the lead mechanical engineer. An older white gentleman, he was quite frugal. Fran only owned four suits, each a different color. Fran was sensible, but he would also yell and scream at staff members when drawings were due to the architect who managed our projects. Although Fran seemed like a tyrant at times, he genuinely cared about all of his employees. Besides taking me to lunch to get to know me, Fran asked me questions about how I grew up and discussed my career aspirations in engineering. He continually challenged me.

One day we were on top of a commercial building—and Fran was wearing one of his four suits. He asked me to climb into a mechanical duct. After he saw the surprised look on my face, he took off his suit jacket and tie and climbed in himself. After climbing out with the proper measurements needed, Fran looked at me and said, just because we're all dressed up, it doesn't mean we can't get dirty from time to time. He never criticized me or made me feel inadequate for my hesitation; he made a simple comment and left it alone. Later on, I learned that Fred's suits were pretty expensive because they were custom-made and dirt resistant. Hence the reason he only owned four.

Another time, my car was parked in the wrong parking spot. When I saw the tow truck, I ran outside to tell him I'd move it, but the tow truck driver already had my car hitched to his truck. I pleaded with the tow truck driver, and he said that because the car was already in the air, it would cost $100 to lower it. Back then, that was a small fortune. I saw a friend walking out of the building, Fran and the second-highest commanding engineer right behind him. They looked like superheroes with their suit jackets blowing in the wind. Just as Fran usually did when he got upset, he yelled at the tow truck driver and demanded that he put down my car. When the driver started to retort, Fran raised his voice. I don't remember what he said precisely, but it went something like this, "If you don't put that car down at this very moment, you'll be looking for a new job tomorrow." I saw the tow truck driver's eyes well up, and I was astonished. I felt sympathy for the tow truck driver because I knew what it was like to be yelled at, and I also felt an enormous sense of belonging.

Although from time to time, Fran yelled at me, along with everyone else, I was sure that he would always be on my side no matter what. Shortly after that incident, I was married to my first wife, and Fran brought his wife to celebrate. Although Fran was a serious, constructive boss, he had a way of poking fun at you to let you know he liked you. The whole team mirrored the same sense of humor.

One day I made a spelling mistake on a mechanical drawing. Instead of spelling the word "duct," a galvanized steel shaft that carries air throughout different building areas, I spelled "duck" (like the bird). Fran went home and told his wife, and she got in on poking fun at me. She purchased a big roll of commercial duct tape, wrapped it, and had Fran stick it on my desk the next morning before I arrived. When I came to work, all of the engineers and designers laughed; they said, this will help you remember to which duct you are referring when you create the drawings.

Those experiences were more than twenty years ago, but I never forget how Fran and the rest of the engineers made me feel. Although I was the only person of color, I felt like I belonged. When I present training at engineering and construction management companies, my audience gets a kick out of hearing my stories about Fran.

Fran was not the nicest person or the easiest person to get along with, but he created an environment where people knew they belonged. Fran was authentic; you knew when he was upset, you knew when he was happy, and you knew when he was trying to teach you a lesson.

The moral of the story is that we all need to be more like Fran. I do not mean yelling at tow truck drivers; I mean really caring for others, especially those who are different from us, being authentic, not just placating or smiling in each other's faces, but genuinely caring and connecting with one another. It's truly the only way to create a culture of belonging. People who value authenticity and inclusion cultivate a sense of belonging that imparts trust and the ability to accomplish amazing feats.

Because class migrants are in the minority, they face a unique challenge in establishing meaningful connections in a corporate environment. When they don't feel socially integrated or part of the corporate social fabric, it can affect emotions, attitudes, and behaviors that trigger covering and psychological erosion. Research indicates that "people with low connectedness often experience loneliness, anxiety, jealousy, anger, depression, low self-esteem, and a host of other negative emotions."[13] These findings underscore the importance of employee belongingness and the far-reaching implications when they don't. It not only affects their physical and psychological health and well-being, but it can also manifest itself in the form of disengagement and a decreased desire to contribute to teams and work objectives.

All employees, whites and nonwhites alike, have a need to belong, which is critical to inclusion, motivation, performance, and retention. Organizations can shape a culture of belonging by developing company-sponsored business resource groups, employee-led resource groups, and formal mentoring, which I describe in chapter 8.

8

Mentorship

The Bridge to Equity

A mentor is a person, an expert in a specific area of endeavor, who trains, guides and observes a less experienced person to also become an expert through support, advice, and involvement in character-building opportunities. —Israelmore Ayivor

Imagine that you are walking down a dark staircase. You cannot see your hands or your feet; you can only hear the voice of a person guiding you. He tells you where to step, how big the step is, and where the railing is so you can hold on without falling. You trust this person because he successfully walked down the same stairs before. And you know that if you stumble, he will catch you. This person is a mentor. This person serves as a light in a dark or unfamiliar environment; his guidance helps you avoid missteps and shows you the quickest route to your destination. From the protégé to the organization, everyone benefits from mentorship. Class migrant mentorships are invaluable. When mentors share their business experience, knowledge, and inside information, it provides class migrants with a road map to advance and a sense of inclusion, equity, and belonging.

GAINING EQUITY THROUGH MENTORSHIP

Before diversity became mainstream, companies and government agencies focused on equal employment opportunity. The Equal Employment Opportunity Commission (EEOC) enforces federal laws. One of them, Title VII of the Civil Rights Act of 1964, makes it illegal to discriminate against a job applicant or an employee because of the person's race, color, religion, sex (including pregnancy, transgender status, and sexual orientation), national origin, age, disability, or genetic information. In the early 1990s, workplace diversity efforts climbed, and by 2013, diversity and inclusion became a business imperative.[1]

At that time, companies focused on diversity or hiring those different from the status quo, and inclusion efforts fell under the umbrella of equal opportunities. Today equity is part of the conversation. If you are unfamiliar with equity as it pertains to the diversity conversation, equity means that you have a fair opportunity, not an equal opportunity.

Equity, also known as fair play or evenhandedness, is critical to understand in terms of upper mobility, both personally and professionally. Here is an example: If you are a hiring manager at a large corporation, and two college graduates from the same school interview for the same position, you might think they are equally equipped. In some cases, this may be true. If one happens to be a class migrant or minority, your assumption may be incorrect. Although the two candidates on paper look similar, their backgrounds may say otherwise. Both may have attended Harvard University, but their backstories are different.

A white person may have had unpaid corporate internships, mentorships, parental advice in career decisions, study abroad programs, or other unseen corporate-world preparations, whereas a person of color may not have had those opportunities.

The class migrant, minority, or person of color likely lacks those valuable opportunities and experiences. These opportunities and experiences seemingly may be small but make a significant difference in the interviewing process when the interviewer asks the job candidates questions about their background or even basic questions such as why they want the position. Some candidates have had parental guidance, circumstances, environments, and substantial time and resources that prepared them for the interview.

That is, under the surface, those who are not minority or class migrants most likely have had some form of mentoring that prepared them for the position. Many class migrants don't have the necessary presentation skills, professional terminology, posture, etiquette, or common hobbies that help candidates build a rapport and likability with white interviewers. Although both meet the requirements for the position, the one who knows the unspoken rules of the corporate world will get the job.

A 2019 study that Yale University conducted revealed that hiring managers tend to hire candidates based on a few seconds of speech during interviews.[2] Some may say this is about race. I would say this is about class or being a class migrant. People feel comfortable with those to whom they can relate, but it is more about your ability to articulate than it is about your skin color. This is where a mentor can make all the difference.

During my first corporate consulting interview, I was underprepared. I had never had a consulting position and knew little about the field or vernacular. My mentor, Dr. Lynn Scott, helped me in three key areas:

1. He explained how to research the company and the people who would interview me.
2. He wrote a glowing letter of recommendation for me.
3. He provided several techniques on how to land the job.

Not only did my mentor give me the tools and insights to obtain the job, but he also helped me navigate the corporate consulting world. Dr. Scott was well equipped to mentor because he had held leadership positions and had years of experience giving presentations.

I met with my mentor once a month to talk about the latest opportunities and challenges. Before the meeting, I prepared questions and concerns for Dr. Scott. He would listen carefully, then provide strategies and concepts to think about and work on until our next meeting. He spoke with me about knowing who holds power when you walk into a room, the right timing to present an idea, being cautious of overstepping bounds, and how to listen for opportunities. These skills, which I had not yet honed, were critical for my upward mobility. Even when leadership in my company tried to discourage me from pursuing my master's in strategic leadership, my mentor ultimately encouraged me—but not without challenging my reasons.

Dr. Scott was instrumental to my success as a consultant. The knowledge and insights he shared with me were valuable gems; they still illuminate my vision and influence my decisions on a daily basis. As a class migrant, I did not have access to mentors with corporate experience while growing up. Mentors shine a light on opportunities that are off your radar, and they teach you the rules of the game even if you don't know what game you're playing. Absent equity and mentorship, you most likely would not be reading this book.

Maybe you want to up your basketball game over the summer to land that college scholarship. Perhaps you're trying to figure out how to get the corner office in a company you have only worked at for two years. Or maybe you want to find out how to land a book contract with a reputable publisher to get your book published. It doesn't matter if you wish to learn the real estate market or get into the NBA. Whatever you want to achieve, the right mentor can help you.

The word mentor originates from Greek mythology. It means to have a trusted counselor, teacher, or wise adviser. Every form of civilization uses mentorship in some form to teach the young or inexperienced. Mentoring is a way to share critical information, motivate, give emotional support, set goals, build contacts, and identify resources.[3] In ancient times, royalty used mentorship to develop their offspring into regal young men and women. In the lower classes, these mentorships were called apprenticeships.

Both mentorships and apprenticeships are designed to develop characteristics and prepare young people to reach their full potential. Apprenticeships focus on developing craftsman and artisan skills for carpenters, fishermen, and other labor-focused careers. Upper-class mentors in homes and communities focus on gentlemanly qualities for men and ladylike qualities for women.

Part of mentorship involves knowing which hat to wear and when—how to negotiate business, how to court a woman, how to act ladylike in public, or how to fence or handle a sword properly. Nowadays, mentors teach a myriad of skills.

FAMOUS MENTORING RELATIONSHIPS

When I first talked to class migrants about mentorships, they thought about volunteers with the Big Brothers or Big Sisters network, someone who would pick them up and take them for ice cream, maybe to a ball game or other activities to keep them out of trouble. This mentoring helps, but it has limits because of the nature of volunteering. Often vulnerable young people don't get a chance to build one-on-one relationships with an individual or mentor who understands and can support or guide their goals, needs, and challenges.

During corporate training workshops, I've asked participants to tell me about a famous person they admire. I then challenge them to read a biography of that person to find out who mentored him or her. In every case, someone supported their success—a parent, family member, teacher, sports coach, college professor, manager, or someone they befriended who took an interest in their success.

Check out these famous mentor relationships:

- Michael Jordan had his father and his coach, Phil Jackson.
- Steve Jobs, the late CEO of Apple, mentored Mark Zuckerberg.
- Former Morehouse College President Dr. Benjamin E. Mays mentored Martin Luther King Jr.
- Bob Dylan's mentor was Woody Guthrie, whose musical legacy includes hundreds of political, traditional, and children's songs, including "This Land Is Your Land."
- Former Super Bowl champ Darrell Green's mentor was his middle-school football coach.
- Fashion designer Christian Dior mentored fellow haute couture designer Yves St. Laurent.
- Former U.S. secretary of state and army general Colin Powell considered his father, Luther Powell, an influential mentor.
- Warren Buffett mentored Microsoft multibillionaire Bill Gates.
- Musician Ray Charles mentored music industry legend Quincy Jones.
- Jacqueline Kennedy Onassis mentored the legendary singer and actress Tina Turner.

Some mentorships occur even when the two people never meet. Sometimes just reading someone's biography and following them in the media can transform your life. And if you're lucky, you eventually get to meet them.

Oprah Winfrey first learned about Maya Angelou when she read *I Know Why the Caged Bird Sings*. Oprah immediately felt connected to her because her life mirrored Angelou's upbringing in the South. She found support because it validated her experiences (I'm OK). Years later, the two met, and the bond was instant. As Oprah says, "She's the woman who can share my triumphs, chide me with hard truth, and soothe me with words of comfort when I call her in my deepest pain." As Oprah Winfrey's relationship with Maya Angelou makes abundantly clear, the supportive leader will be there for you, but also tell you the "hard truth," provide needed guidance, and help you get to the next level.[4] —Glenn and Michael Parker, *Positive Influence*

When I first started speaking, I followed Les Brown, a world-renowned motivational speaker who went from abject poverty to multimillionaire. I eventually met Les. He helped me "make up my mind to become unstoppable"; to become a "no matter what person," as he said.[5] Willie Jolley, Les's mentee, became my mentor and wrote the foreword to my second self-published book, *Seeds of Greatness*. Even though they are deceased, I have used several people as vicarious mentors, including Frederick Douglass, Madam C. J. Walker, Harriet Tubman, and Napoleon Hill, author of *Think and Grow Rich*. It's really about self-mentoring: I read their books, watch their videos, listen to their audio programs, and have conversations about them as if I know them.

Ekaterina Dyspikinam, an immigrant I interviewed in 2021, was raised on a farm in a small Russian village. When she arrived in the United States, a mentor helped her navigate American culture. Podcasts and YouTube helped Ekaterina identify her passions, her why, and it opened a pathway to information and mentorship. Ekaterina said mentors could "push you and hold you accountable to the person that you say that you want to be. Not, just say that 'Hey, this is what I want to do. This is where I want to be.'"

> But what are the steps, because sometimes the steps are hard. And sometimes the growth happens through the uncomfortable and through the hard times . . . the advice that I have received helped me to better myself and let go to the next level, [*sic*] value where I am at today, and instilled a sense of there is nothing you can't do . . . That was important for me because it basically made me a problem solver that made me not take no for an answer . . . I learned not to run from tough situations. I learned to solve them, and that is a big achievement of the mentors that I had. Whether it is an actual person, or it is

an author, or the podcasts, [*sic*] it definitely enriched my life in many, many ways.[6]

Ekaterina became a forever learner. "That is why," as she said, "I am being mentored by all these podcasts, and I read books on self-improvement, and growth, and development, and I have attended some of the conferences as well on the topic." Ekaterina was a teenager when she arrived in the United States but could not speak English at that time. After earning her high school diploma, she attended SUNY Brockport and graduated with a bachelor's in international studies and political science. Today, Ekaterina is an executive assistant at Capital One.

Later in this chapter, I'll share some tips on how to approach the partnership of mentoring. These techniques will help you find mentors you know, don't know, or who passed on before you were ever born.

HOW MENTORING CAN LEAD TO BELONGING

Although my father was always in my life, my mentors have filled in the gaps. Absent mentorship, I would be lost because I've had so many challenges and experiences that my biological father could not understand or support. One of the most significant challenges class migrants have is not feeling like they belong. Some experience alienation when they move into a new environment, social class, or occupation. A mentor can soften that feeling of alienation. Even if your mentor is not a class migrant, he can understand your challenges because you've built an intimate relationship with him. Before we go further, know that mentors are not created equally.

I have had mentors of different races, genders, religions, social class, and industries. Some were more effective than others. Some could only take me so far. Some were hard on me; others were empathetic. Vicki Hess, keynote speaker and author, mentored me for a while. She was a no-nonsense white woman who recommended that I cut my dreadlocks. Some people take suggestions like this to heart. Some may even think that the recommendation was racist. But as a mentor, she definitely was not racist; she was merely looking out for me because she knows the game and its rules. If a blonde-haired woman has pink streaks in her hair, Vicki probably

would tell her to ditch it; otherwise, people may not take her seriously. Today's corporate environment is more accepting when it
comes to cultural and style diversity.

Howard Ross, the founder of Cook Ross, breaks down the rationale behind workplace appearance. Fifteen years ago, Howard mentored college students. Here is his advice to one African American
Stanford undergrad named Brian.

> Brian is very smart, very dark skin and a big guy; he was a football
> player . . . applying for a job, and he had his hair in twists. He came
> to me to get coaching for his job interview. He said, "Do you think I
> should cut my hair?" I said, "Look, Brian, here's how I feel about it.
> I like your hair; I think it looks great on you. It would not bother me
> even a little bit. I think it looks great." I said, "and there are some
> people who are going to react to it. So the question you have to ask
> yourself, Brian, is how important is it to you. If you are willing to take
> the risk of somebody using that as a disqualifier because you believe
> that is your identity, then I say keep your hair the way it is. If it is just
> a way you have your hair, like just the shirt you are wearing today or
> just a particular hairstyle you got, then you might want to cut it and
> not let it get in the way. But it is totally your choice, and there is no
> right or wrong about it."
>
> "Do not go up to the hot stove and touch the hot stove and then
> curse the stove because you knew it was hot; you know what is there.
> So if you are going to go in there, be responsible for it. That is my best
> coaching for you. Be responsible for that choice. If your choice is, 'I am
> only going to work someplace where I can express this part of myself,'
> God bless you. That is totally appropriate. You have the right to do
> that. But if somebody else says, 'I do not want somebody working for
> me who expresses themselves that way,' that is also their choice. So do
> not then be a victim about it."[7]

Mentors tell you the hard truth. That's what you need; that's what
you want. Mentorship is not about appeasing someone. Although
eventually you may become friends with a mentor, it's not about
friendship. Mentoring is a professional relationship. Some mentors
are expressive; others may not explain the reasons or intent behind
their advice. But one thing I've learned is not to take things personally. Mentors are there to show you what they know—listen carefully and look at their advice as an opportunity to grow. The minute
you take offense, you go off track and on defense. Although we take
things with a grain of salt outside mentorship, we must trust the

process inside it. Growing is a journey. Howard also taught me a lot about social dynamics and the importance of asking questions without fear and prejudgment.

> One of the things I would say to people who are class migrants is that class, like any other divisions we talked about, gets established in an inside-outside way. There is the in-group, and there is the out-group. The in-group obviously are the people who are wealthier, right. But whenever we have in-group out-group, we have that dynamic of what's been called the "out-group homogeneity effect." You tend to think of them as all the same. So, it is like wealthy people think of poor people as being kind of all the same and poor people think of wealthy people as kind of being all the same. And so, a lot of times people will come up to somebody like me, and they see me to a later stage of my career after I built this big company and I got fifty people working for me, and I am driving a Tesla and all this stuff, and they think, "Well, you will never understand what my life was about." Whereas the truth is, I may very well understand it because of my life experience, because of my father's life experience, because of the other people I have worked with within communities that were really underserved and under-resourced. As a result of that, sometimes people did not come to me for the kind of support that I could provide them because they were afraid that I would be looking down on them.[8]

Mentors can provide strategies and stretch opportunities that take you out of your comfort zone, and they can mean the difference between being hired or being disqualified.

> The ultimate measure of a man is not where he stands in moments of comfort and convenience but where he stands at times of challenge and controversy. —Martin Luther King Jr.

It's essential to have mentors who differ from you. Looking back, Vicki and Howard could not have been more different from me. They are both older, white, and had a very different upbringing than me.

Vicki let me shadow her at a speaking engagement to see firsthand how she rocked the crowd. It was inspiring to see her dance on stage, and although she didn't have the greatest rhythm, she knew it and didn't care. She danced, and her audience loved it. Vicki taught me the importance of being yourself, but she also taught me to know your audience. Meaning: I learned when to leave some of my personality at the door to get my foot in the door. Realize that there's a delicate balance between being authentic and being professional. After all, even if we grew up in a culture where everyone wore leather pants and large nose rings, it does not mean wearing them to work is appropriate business attire, and it does not make you any less authentic if you don't. In the workplace, if you want to be authentic, focus on staying true to your values (integrity, honesty, reliability); hair and clothing are stylistic choices. Until you know your audience and they know you, it's best to follow company social norms, as long as they're ethical. Over the years, these insights have helped me succeed.

WHY DOES MENTORING WORK?

Consider mentoring an investment. An investment requires time and attention. Time is the most valuable commodity. Most people do not value their time, but the successful do. When seeking a mentor, think of it like a trip to a bank to ask for a business loan. Banks don't give just anyone a loan; they need to see your plan. They want to know if you have collateral and you are a good investment. So do mentors. Even if you don't have a great plan, mentors want to know your specific desire, a goal you want to accomplish, and your initial game plan, even if it's not a good one.

Mentors will not waste their time with someone who does not listen, has not or is unwilling to do prep work or legwork. Understanding the mentor-mentee dynamic is imperative. Dr. Scott once said, "This relationship isn't just about you; it's about me, too." He meant that our relationship was symbiotic, so we both received a reward, given the information he shared with me. The return on his investment was to see my success; he helped me climb the corporate ladder, and I hope my success has helped him live out part of his legacy.

Mentors expect you to listen to their advice. When I began to earn more money, I wanted to buy a new Tesla, but Dr. Scott told me to wait; that time would come. I took his advice and instead purchased a two-year-old Audi. Scaling back was not easy. At the time, it was against my desire, but it allowed me to save a lot of money, which was his plan from the start. Sometimes our ambitions can get the best of us. This experience taught me the value of thinking long-term and strategically—not to let impulses, emotions, and short-term thinking drive my decision making.

Dr. Scott didn't just help me with personal finances. He told me to set up a meeting with one of the vice presidents of the company. He asked, "What does she like to do?" I said, "She likes to take photos with her drone." He said, "Well, then you should buy a drone."[9] I purchased the drone, learned to fly it, and scheduled time with the vice president to fly the drone during a lunch break. It made for a great conversation and segued into further discussions about my position and goals within the company. In 2019, after company layoffs, she moved on to chief diversity officer at CarMax, but we remain great friends to this day. Why? Because we flew drones together. Mentors can teach you how to build networks and bridges with influential people, which is key to opening doors.

BE VIGILANT, OPEN, AND READY FOR NEW OPPORTUNITIES

You must be ready to receive the investment of time from a potential mentor. What do I mean by ready? You must be prepared to work hard, listen closely, ask insightful questions, and follow recommendations, such as reading books, learning new activities, and following up. If your mentor gives you a contact to call or e-mail, make sure you do it. Mentors are no different than you or me when it comes to time; they have limits and pet peeves.

In some cases, your mentor will test you to see if you are serious and willing to take the extra steps. You must show more than interest and curiosity. You must commit and be definitive about the process. Once you have passed a mentor's test, he will be willing to devote his time, and then you can drink from his knowledge. If you do not pass the test, you'll know because the relationship will stall.

When I first began to speak at events, I was supposed to partner with Vance, an esteemed veteran who spoke at military bases around the country. He asked me to make a couple of phone calls to secure a venue. I was reluctant because it felt intimidating, as I had never done that before. After three requests, Vance stopped taking my calls. I learned this lesson the hard way. Sometimes mentors are not a good match for you or for that point in your career growth. It is essential to assess where you are, where you want to go, and what you're ready to take on. If you're looking for a job, you don't need a mentor at the CEO level. Finding the right mentor is half the battle.

You need a mentor to push you beyond your comfort zone to some degree, but the challenges she presents must be appropriate for your stage of development.

HOW TO FIND A MENTOR

At my professional development presentations, I always advise people to get a mentor, and they always ask how to find one. Although the stories I share can make finding a mentor seem easy, I realize that it can take some effort. Being a people person and engaged in personal development for almost twenty years has helped me tremendously. However, I would not advise you to walk up to just anyone on the street and ask her to mentor you. The best approach to finding a mentor is to attend conferences, talk to the speakers, join industry groups and associations, and seek thought leaders in your field. I've also found some of my best mentors on airplanes, at college, at work, and at my church and spiritual center in random meetings. The point is to keep your eyes open for mentorship opportunities.

Bob Baker, whom I mentioned in chapter 3, is one of my oldest mentor relationships. Bob came to my house to share information about a life insurance policy and a mutual fund. Shortly after speaking with him, I realized that he was the owner of the company that I had previously sought to help fund a nonprofit I had started years back. During our conversation, Bob's eyes zeroed in on one book on my shelf, *Think and Grow Rich* by Napoleon Hill. Our conversation shifted from insurance quotes to book quotes. Bob wanted to know if I had read the book and what I had learned. After peppering me with questions, which I gladly answered as I had recently finished reading the book, Bob invited me to lunch, and the rest is history. Looking back, I believe that Bob saw my book collection, initiatives, and passion when describing Hill's wealth principles and practices. In other words, he invested in me because he saw that I was invested in personal and professional growth.

Again, mentorships don't always come that easily. You must be intentional about where you want to go in your personal and/or professional life. Remember, a mentor is investing in you. If you have no direction, the mentor won't see a high return on investment.

Over the years, I have declined to mentor certain individuals for that exact reason.

THE MENTORSHIP RESPONSIBILITY

Mentoring is a mutual responsibility. It is a responsibility for the mentor as well as the mentee. A genuine mentor relationship should be consistent and impactful. As I mentioned earlier, self-mentorships can and should occur through books, and video and audio programs in addition to mentoring. Some will be a one-time conversation. But the best mentor relationships happen when you can ask the person questions specific to your situation, and he answers from the place where you are today. Books and audio programs are what I refer to as self-mentorships or supplemental personal development, but they need to be followed by face-to-face mentorships. The primary responsibility of a mentorship lies on the shoulders of the mentee. If you guessed that this is because of the time commitment, you guessed right.

OBJECTIVES FOR THE MENTEE

Your initial objective is to write your goals, read books, and watch informative videos in your area of interest. This process is part of the journey; you will continue to self-mentor and refine your goals before and after finding a mentor.

The second objective involves using your goals to develop a script. You'll use it to pitch your idea and the reasons why someone should mentor you. A mentor needs to be inspired by your desire to grow. After all, if you aren't motivated to develop yourself, you'll never inspire someone else to mentor you. I'll never forget when Howard Ross told me, "One of the things that I always appreciate about your relationship and my relationship with you was that you were so open to coaching. From day one, you were like a sponge, and that is inspiring."[10]

The third objective is talent discovery. Each of us has raw, untapped talent; the right mentor will see it and help you shape it. When a mentor sees your talent and your burning desire for success, or your willingness to work with what you have, she will be more apt to take a leap of faith and invest her time in you. From that point on, she has taken responsibility for her part of the mentor relationship—now, the real learning begins.

> We're better investors when we bring diverse perspectives and experiences to the table. More inclusive teams function better and make us a better employer too, especially as we strive to recruit younger generations who care deeply about how we engage with society. —Sonny Kalsi, co-CEO, BentallGreenOak

WHY SHOULD COMPANIES DEVELOP MENTORING PROGRAMS?

Mentoring is an investment. Smart, progressive companies know it. A 2019 mentoring article published by Gloat says, "70% of Fortune 500 companies implementing mentoring programs are increasingly recognized as a smart business investment."[11] Mentoring is one of the most efficient ways for a company to develop its talent pool. The article highlights the mentoring programs of five companies: Caterpillar, Schneider Electric, Bain and Company, General Electric (GE), and Fidelity Investments. Mentoring programs provide employees with experiences that help to develop future leaders and increase employee retention.

In 2008 I was hired as a community engagement coordinator for a medium-size Washington, D.C., nonprofit. During my interview, I asked the executive director if mentoring would be part of my development in the company. He looked puzzled, like this was the first time he had been asked this question. He said, "No." Then I was puzzled because I wondered how I would develop my leadership skills.

During my tenure at the nonprofit, I experienced numerous leadership challenges that I was not equipped to handle. One specific situation involved managing six employees, one of whom turned out to be a nice guy, but he refused to work. It didn't matter who hired this guy, which often crossed my mind, but he was in my department, so he was my responsibility. For the life of me, I could not find a way to motivate him. I didn't have the knowledge, emotional intelligence, or communication skills to engage him effectively. We had many fallouts. No matter what approach I tried, he didn't become productive. Eventually, he left the company of his own accord.

If I had known then what I know now, I could have managed the situation better. A mentor would have been able to give me the tools to understand my weaknesses and develop my strengths to lead this employee effectively or at least manage the process better to get him a position within the company where he could excel. Sometimes that better place is on the other side of the door. Either way, mentoring would've helped.

Ten years later, in 2018, I worked for a contract training company, Fred Pryor. As a trainer, I flew across the United States, delivering management and leadership skills training to mid-level managers in various industries. The coaching segment of the training was noteworthy. We talked about management skills versus leadership skills, how to communicate and manage up. Most of the attendees were impressed after I shared a few essential strategies for leading employees and managing projects. It was as if it was a newfangled concept, like no one had ever taught them the difference between leadership and management. When I asked if they had mentors, I received blank stares. Although a lot of companies use mentoring, many don't. Most of the time, I found that it's not because they don't want to be mentored. Rather, they don't know how to engage in mentoring, or the company has not set up a mentoring program.

Ironically, my training participants number one request is that their company start, fund, and continually support a corporate mentorship program. A formal mentoring program is not complicated, but it does require time, strategy, and funding. If companies understood the return on investment of mentoring as GE and Fidelity Investments do organizational change, they would hire an outside consultant or partner with a nonprofit to help develop their procedures.

DEVELOPING CORPORATE MENTORING PROGRAMS

Organizations should view mentoring programs as an investment and a benefit they can offer to employees. Mentoring should not be merely informal or on a volunteer basis. A corporate-sponsored mentorship should be showcased as a privilege because it adds value to the company, the mentor, and the mentee. Organizations should not attempt to develop a formal mentoring program if leadership is not supportive. Mentoring programs require resources and dedication and should be measured and integrated into the overarching objective.

Although we would like to think all people are altruistic and willing to take the time to mentor others, this is not realistic. Often people sit on boards, especially nonpaid boards, or volunteer with Habitat for Humanity because it looks good on their résumé, and it can be considered prestigious. Ideally, organizations want employees and candidates to see their mentoring program as an opportunity to make an impact and be among the elite. Doing so will attract the best talent and people in the company to participate. When you get high-level leaders onboard, you also get high-level employees who want to make a difference—and that is necessary for the program's success. Although this differs for nonprofits, the focus is on success and stature in the competitive corporate world. Again, although we want to believe that people should want to give their time freely, and many do, they also want the best return on investment for themselves and others. Failing to consider this concept when planning your mentoring program could jeopardize the entire program.

A mentoring program requires a plan similar to a business plan. And, if organizations want their program to succeed, they *should not* start it on a shoestring. After delivering numerous training workshops across the country, I've found that they take some time to implement and refine.

As 2019 came to an end, I reviewed all the client strategies my workshop participants suggested at the end of each training session. The number one strategy for creating a more inclusive environment in the workplace was mentorship. Half of the companies said they had tried but failed to develop a mentorship program. The other half either had informal mentorships or never attempted to develop a formal program because they could not procure buy-in from leadership.

The most successful mentoring program that I have come across was a midsize financial firm located in Manhattan, New York. Its mentoring program is succinct, supported from the top down, well funded, and considered an exclusive hub for seasoned and junior-level leaders.

The process is simple. When an employee qualifies for the program, he has access to three different C-suite leaders (including the chief executive officer) of his choice for six weeks. This program took mentoring to a whole new level. Mentoring is embedded in the organization's fabric rather than mentors carving time out of their schedules for mentees.

Leaders do not just meet with the mentees for lunch; they bring them into their meetings, strategy calls, and even take them to pick their children up after work. Doing so allows the mentees to understand firsthand what it takes to be a leader. It's similar to shadowing, but more intensive, and it enables the leader to continue his day with few interruptions. Depending on work and travel schedules, the mentee can shadow the leader for a couple of hours or a whole day.

The mentee prepares by writing down questions to ask at the end of the day or the next time they meet. The program includes designated office monitors who write company news highlights to acknowledge graduates and keep it top of mind for those interested. Once mentees graduate from the program, the company gives them an honorary pin to signify that they have been a part of this experience. Subsequently, they are eligible to mentor new employees.

The company created a short application process where women, men, and non-binary alike were accepted to participate as mentors or mentees. Admittedly, far fewer women, minorities, and non-binary are at the leadership level. But developing a pool of underrepresented employees that leadership could consider for succession planning is one of the most significant reasons for a mentorship program.

This program also comprises a screening method that disqualifies people who are not serious or ready to be a mentor or mentee. The program is available to employees on a separate company website. Anyone can access the landing page and review it, but only employees who are members can gain access.

Together, these things make the mentorship program exclusive. To ensure that the program accommodates minorities, managers can nominate mentees who show high potential but need polishing. At the time, the firm's minority quota was 30 percent.

Participants who graduate from the mentorship program ultimately see leadership and the company through a new lens. Working side by side with different seasoned mentors provides a personalized experience and a 360-degree view of the organization, which accelerates learning, development, and job satisfaction.

Mentees learn the inner workings of the business and its operations. They gain clarity about the value of their work and how it contributes to the final product, which makes work more meaningful, improves engagement and performance, gives a sense of ownership and a visible stake in the outcome. Mentees also learn how to communicate, negotiate, and resolve conflict effectively. Mentors help mentees understand both everyday and broader issues the company faces as they observe leaders and their daily responsibilities, including handling tough decisions for the company's greater good.

Given the guidance, support, feedback, and stretch opportunities, program graduates feel like stakeholders rather than employees. They build constructive relationships, make wiser decisions, align with company objectives, and advance more quickly. In turn, productivity increases, and costly mistakes, absenteeism, and disengagement decrease.

Over time, company communication begins to flow vertically and horizontally, laying a solid foundation for increased knowledge-sharing, divergent ideas, cooperation, teamwork, and commitment to the organization.

Mentorship goes beyond personal and professional development. It decreases biases and increases diversity, inclusion, equity, cultural and social capital for class migrants and minorities, which bridges the gap between social classes and helps class migrants assimilate to the social norms and social class they aspire to join.

Graduates also exhibit higher levels of empathy, emotional intelligence, and problem-solving skills. All in all, this company had cracked the code on developing a successful mentorship program. The program is operational in quarter stints rather than year-round, which aligns with leaders' schedules. Although mentors make themselves available throughout the year, their obligation is minimal because it has a foreseeable beginning and end. And the time frames also help to manage mentees' expectations.

Some corporations sponsor annual mentorship programs on a rotational basis. Different departments within the organization are required to leave open a certain number of spots for mentorship. Employees must apply for mentee spots, but they typically spend a year working with another leader to learn the leadership landscape and business from different angles. Mentees can rotate to the IT department, marketing, finance, human resources, production, finance, or supply chain management. Although these usually are lateral positions, the leaders, diverse fields of exposure, and business insights prepare protégés for top leadership positions.

Here are some steps to consider when developing a corporate mentorship program.

EIGHT MENTORSHIP STEPS TO GARNER CORPORATE LEADERSHIP BUY-IN

Location, location, location! Realtors know this mantra well. They know people do not necessarily buy homes based merely on the size of property or aesthetics. People purchase homes because of the location, schools, neighborhood, nearby fresh produce, commute to work, and the status that comes with it. Those developing a plan for formal mentorship should have a similar thought process. A mentorship mantra should be value, value, value! Just as people purchase homes for location, people create and participate in mentorship programs because of the value.

Step 1—State Your Purpose

Create an executive summary that clearly and concisely states the purpose of the mentorship program. It could be to develop a talent pool for succession planning, risk management, or to attract, engage, and retain more diverse talent. Whatever your purpose, it needs to be clearly defined and communicated. A passionate mentoring committee is good because it helps rally others. But the CFO, shareholders, and other stakeholders are more likely to support an initiative with a solid business plan that holds validity and demonstrates the value added to the organization. Some of these include increased engagement and productivity, innovation, creating equity, a diverse and inclusive culture, bringing aboard minority leadership representative of employees and customers, cost savings, improved reputation, and competitive advantage.

Step 2—Form a Mentorship Committee

In the initial stages, it's helpful to form a mentorship committee, perform preliminary research, and work out the details and challenges with someone who has developed an effective mentorship program. If you don't know someone in the company with experience, you can hire a consultant or begin by making a comprehensive list of all the benefits for both leaders and mentees in the program. Put budget concerns aside until this is fully fleshed out. Remember, a business plan is more than metrics and statistics; people must understand the program's value and their personal return on investment.

Step 3—Educate, Survey, and Gain Input

Provide information on the company website and hold meetings to educate leaders and employees about formal mentorship, then develop an initial questionnaire and survey leaders and employees to understand how much interest there is in the program. Ask for input and recommendations from leaders because including them in decision making will motivate them to participate, share ideas, commit their time, and support the budget.

Step 4—Evaluate Cost Benefits

Perform a cost-benefit analysis. Evaluate current business expenses such as disengagement, absenteeism, retention/turnover, preventable mistakes, and failed or noneffective ethical, safety, inclusion, diversity, equity and access, and leadership/EQ training efforts. Understand the benefits and values of the mentorship program and translate them into a cost reduction/savings plan (i.e., mentoring increases empathy and emotional intelligence organically because of the relationships formed between class migrants and leaders).

As mentioned, mentorship programs are effective when they are woven into the company fabric. Your proposal should not only align the mentoring program with the annual budget but be embedded in your IDEA initiatives and leadership training and development strategy. Because a formal mentoring program is high touch, its benefits positively influence and reach across every corporate function (it also increases transparency and mitigates silos of knowledge). As your committee prepares the mentorship proposal for the HR executive who reports to the CEO, include mentoring statistics from authoritative sources that reveal increases in productivity, engagement, retention, employee and customer satisfaction, innovation, logistics, service uptime, and sales. As the program unfolds, use your original internal metrics for a benchmark, then measure these key performance indicators for progress in your IDEA, professional development, and mentoring objectives.

Step 5—Proposal and Presentation

Develop a proposal that delineates the value for the mentor, mentee, and the organization. Include the goals and objectives of the mentorship program, survey and budget analysis results, current expenditures, capital needs, and cost savings projections. Also, consider developing an outline of a pilot program to illustrate the program's implementation process.

Leaders who have experienced formal or informal mentorship will likely understand the value of the program. However, be prepared to educate and explain all the benefits of a formal mentoring program to those who have not had a formal mentor or hold outdated beliefs that mentoring occurs naturally based on their experience.

Approach this like any other business plan. Part of the strategy is knowing your audience, their interests and resistances, dispelling myths, and demonstrating the personal and organizational value to frame the program in a way that encourages executive buy-in.

Step 6—Structure and Management

Structure and management are critical. Every house requires structure and a foundation; your mentorship program is no different.

- Confirm whether the program will be mandatory or voluntary.
- Determine the delivery platform. Although face-to-face is ideal, your organization could facilitate the program via Zoom sessions, Microsoft Teams, or another medium.
- Clarify the duration of the program and the number of mentors and mentees who can be paired at any given time.
- Decide on demographic requirements such as age, gender, race, ethnicity, language, sexual orientation, or department.
- Establish whether you will hold an orientation upon participant acceptance into the program. (Doing so sets expectations and helps prepare mentees with goals and milestones.)

- Define geographical locations that will offer the program; this may be offices in other countries with different cultures.
- Ascertain whether a support team is required to assist mentees or program coordinators.

Other questions to consider: Will you have mentees sign a nondisclosure agreement to maintain confidentiality or provide classified access to secure areas and data? Can employees use their volunteer hours to opt in to the program? How will manager approval work? Will your mentorship program be connected to an internship feeder program or performance goals and reviews? Will you offer a bonus, career mapping, or make tuition reimbursement contingent upon completing the program to incentivize participation? Will you follow the mentorship program with formal training for mentees? Will you invest in training your mentors? Consider all the bells and whistles of the program to determine resources, challenges, and recurring costs.

RESOURCES TO SUPPORT MENTORSHIP PROGRAM

Here are five software companies that can support your company's mentorship program:

1. *eMentorConnect* is a top-rated mentoring, training, and coaching platform best suited for enterprises and large companies and organizations. Leading companies trust their services, including UPS, Johnson & Johnson, and Bayer.
2. *Qooper* works with companies, universities, and nonprofits to surround employees/students with the right mentors, peers, groups, and resources from an automated administration dashboard.
3. *Chronus* offers mentoring software that powers successful programs that impact key metrics for the world's largest organizations and Fortune 50 companies.
4. *Graduway*, known as your three-in-one virtual community, recruits and mentors students, engages alumni, and cultivates donors.
5. *PushFar* is a top mentoring platform accessed via Web and mobile apps. It has helped hundreds of organizations

streamline programs through matching, management, engagement, and in-depth reporting.
6. *my2be* serves tech companies and talent teams. It can quickly launch, manage, and measure inclusive mentoring programs for teams working anywhere.

Step 7—Participant Incentives and Recognition

Organizations must consider the profile of the ideal mentors and mentees. Once a company identifies who it will involve in the program, it can add desirable perks. Some businesses offer bonuses, gift cards, acknowledgment ceremonies and dinners, or announcements on the company website or newsletter. Other companies provide program memorabilia, completion certificates, a company retreat, stretch opportunities, free personality or work-style assessments, or a combination of awards. These are just some of the benefits to think about offering participants. When it comes to incentives and rewards, quality tops quantity. Offering fewer but more impactful accolades and honorary awards will attract industrious participants to take part in your mentorship program.

Step 8—Marketing

Consider promoting and building a brand around your mentorship program. Use social media and the company intranet for marketing to attract external high-growth-needs candidates and internal participation. Mention the program in job descriptions, recruiting, selection, and onboarding processes—some companies instruct managers to speak about the mentorship program at staff meetings. YouTube and podcasts are effective ways to highlight mentee accomplishments and increase program visibility. After some success, you could ask graduates to write positive testimonials, or your program could be featured in the news.

MENTORSHIP IN A NUTSHELL

Mentorship is beneficial to the mentee, mentor, and organization. In chapter 1, I spoke about scaffolding and how each of us needs it to support our growth and success. Remember what John said:

To say that I am where I am today because of my own doing, my own effort, my own merits—*alone*—is to say that my grandparents, parents, wife, professors, mentors, colleagues, friends, and managers played no part in my success. When in fact, each served me—invested in me and supplied their time, energy, support, connections, and knowledge— giving me the opportunity to perform well, be productive and climb the corporate ladder.[12]

Mentorship is scaffolding for all employees, especially class migrants and minorities. On the one hand, mentorship decreases biases, conflict, and racial tension, disengagement, absenteeism, and turnover. On the other hand, mentorship increases engagement, productivity, awareness, empathy, communication, inclusion, diversity, equity, and access. It also increases cultural capital, a sense of belonging, influential networks, and upward social and career mobility for the mentee. Mentorships break down barriers and provide new perspectives for mentors.

No single leadership course exists that can offer immersive cultural learning experiences; mitigate stereotypes, biases, and alienation; and build a bridge to equity in an organization more effectively than a mentorship program.

Endgame

We've come to the final chapter in this book which I call "Endgame." Endgame typically describes the final stage of a chess match where players must decide how to utilize their final pieces with a few moves. I've entitled this last conversation endgame because I would like you to think about how to best leverage what you've learned in this book to make a few moves that can make all the difference in your career, your life, and the lives of others. Think about what you have read in the previous chapters and reflect on what resonates, challenges, and inspires you. Identify three or more goals you want to achieve based on the stories, strategies, and insights you have gained throughout the chapters, then develop subgoals and a short- and long-term plan to achieve your objectives. Type it up, write it on paper or a napkin, whatever you do, put it to ink, and think outside the box.

To get you started, ask yourself, are there people you have never quite understood because of your own zip code story? Are there places that hold cultural experiences and awareness that you've never visited? Are there things you would like to have, such as an expanded education, a different wardrobe, a trip to a foreign country, an advanced vocabulary, a diverse group of friends or coworkers, or maybe learning a new language? I'm willing to bet there are. If so, consider how you currently show up for people, places, and things and how you can transform how you experience people, places, and things? Focusing on these specific areas can help you change your zip code story.

I hope the interviews and passages in this book sharpen your insights about yourself and others. One thing is for sure; you won't have to read between the lines; each example illuminates how we think, live, and strive for success in business and life. The words and anecdotes capture the realities and experiences of class migrants and aim to broaden the lens of your outlooks and thus your personal and professional lives. Despite your race, ethnicity, sexual orientation, religion, or where or how you grew up, The zip code story holds valuable knowledge, ideas, and practices for everyone.

No matter what adversities and challenges life has thrown you, opportunities exist each time you expand your zip code story. We can increase progress and possibilities by making an effort to meet different people, understand their stories, travel to new places, and try different things. The strategies I've presented can help managers and class migrants start symbiotic conversations and create effective plans that benefit all.

In closing, I urge you to answer one final question:

How will your zip code story impact the people
you meet as you journey through life?

The answer to this question will be determined by what you do next to expand your zip code story.

Notes

CHAPTER 1

1. 50 Cent and Robert Greene, *The 50th Law*, 2009.

2. Reginald F. Lewis and Blair Walker, "The Higher Education of the Late Reginald F. Lewis," *Journal of Blacks in Higher Education*, no. 8 (1995): 84–87, doi:10.2307/2963061 (accessed March 29, 2021).

3. Mary Follin, "Celebrating a Legacy: Father and Son Share Insights at Special Event," *GW Alumni News*, July 12, 2016, www.gwalumni.org/2016/06/celebrating-a-legacy-father-and-son-to-share-insights-at-special-event/.

4. Kim Clark and Ian Johnson, "TOUGH ENOUGH: Jean Fugett's Toughest Job Yet: Replacing Brother Reginald Lewis at TLC Beatrice," baltimoresun.com, January 31, 1993, http://www.baltimoresun.com/news/bs-xpm-1993-01-31-1993031121-story.html (accessed October 24, 2018).

5. National Association of School Psychologists, *Understanding Race and Privilege* (handout) (Bethesda, MD: author, 2016).

6. C. Chen, "On the Shoulders of Giants," in *Mapping Scientific Frontiers: The Quest for Knowledge Visualization* (London: Springer, 2003), https://doi.org/10.1007/978-1-4471-0051-5_5.

7. Gross, Christopher J., and John, Time and resources and their possible constraints on opportunity from John's perspective, personal communication, June 20, 2020.

8. "Thurgood Marshall—A Century of Upstanders," https://sites.google.com/a/ntfh.cmsdnet.net/a-century-of-upstanders2/your-person-s-name/civil-rights-era/thurgood-marshall (accessed March 30, 2021).

9. Joan C. Williams, Marina Multhaup, and Sky Mihaylo, "Why Companies Should Add Class to Their Diversity Discussions," *Harvard Business Review*, September 5, 2018, https://hbr.org/2018/09/why-companies -should-add-class-to-their-diversity-discussions.

10. Holly Yan, "What We Know So Far in the College Admissions Cheating Scandal," *CNN*, March 19, 2019, www.cnn.com/2019/03/13/us/what -we-know-college-admissions-cheating-scandal/index.html.

11. Paul M. Muchinsky, "The Power and Influence Approach," in *Psychology Applied to Work: An Introduction to Industrial and Organizational Psychology*, 10th ed. (Summerfield, NC: Hypergraphic Press, 2012), 401–2.

12. Alice Walker, "The Most Common Way People Give Up Their Power Is by Thinking They Don't Have Any," Good News Network, March 10, 2021, https://www.goodnewsnetwork.org/alice-walker-quote -about-power/.

13. The term "class migrant" was coined by Joan C. Williams in her book, *White Working Class: Overcoming Class Cluelessness in America* (Boston, MA: Harvard Business Review Press, 2017).

14. 50 Cent, and Robert Greene, *The 50th Law*. New York: HarperCollins Publishers, 2009.

15. Michael W. Kraus, Jun Won Park, and Jacinth J. Tan, "Signs of Social Class: The Experience of Economic Inequality in Everyday Life," *Perspectives on Psychological Science* 12, no. 3 (2017): 422–35, https://doi.org/ 10.1177/1745691616673192.

16. Thomas Bachhuber, "NetWorking: Rich Is More Than Money," Center for Life Transitions, March 19, 2019, https://www.centerforlifetransi tions.net/2013/networking-rich-is-more-than-money/#:~:text=Robert%20 Kiyosaki%20says%2C%20%E2%80%9CThe%20richest,because%20they%20 have%20a%20job.

17. Edmond, Alfred, "Earl Graves Said It: Success Principles from the Founder of Black Enterprise." Black Enterprise. Black Enterprise, April 20, 2020. https://www.blackenterprise.com/earl-graves-said-it-business-and -life-success-principles-from-the-founder-of-black-enterprise/.

18. Anonymous, "If you can't see it, you can't be it" (accessed August 4, 2017).

19. Katy O'Donnell, "Leslie Sword's Vision," baltimoresun.com, October 27, 2018, https://www.baltimoresun.com/news/bs-xpm-2007-12-02 -0711220087-story.html.

20. Mary Carole McCauley, "Reginald Lewis' Daughter Opens Up about Growing Up with Her Famous Father," baltimoresun.com, June 19, 2018, https://www.baltimoresun.com/entertainment/arts/bs-ae-lewis-memoir -20120210-story.html.

21. Robert T. Kiyosaki, "Rich Dad Poor Dad: With Updates for Today's World—and 9 New Study Session Sections," 2017, https://www.amazon .com/Rich-Dad-Poor-Teach-Middle/dp/1612680194.

22. Williams, Multhaup, and Mihaylo, "Why Companies Should Add Class to Their Diversity Discussions."

23. Dana Wilkie, "Employers Say Students Aren't Learning Soft Skills in College," SHRM, February 28, 2020, www.shrm.org/resourcesandtools/hr -topics/employee-relations/pages/employers-say-students-arent-learning -soft-skills-in-college.aspx.

CHAPTER 2

1. 50 Cent and Robert Greene, *The 50th Law*, 2009.

2. Rob Cross and Robert J. Thomas, "Managing Yourself: A Smarter Way to Network," *Harvard Business Review*, September 7, 2017, https://hbr .org/2011/07/managing-yourself-a-smarter-way-to-network.

3. Nick Romano, "Jimmy Kimmel Comes to Terms with His Own White Privilege," EW.com, June 3, 2020, https://ew.com/tv/jimmy-kimmel -white-privilege/ (accessed March 29, 2021).

4. National Association of School Psychologists, Understanding Race and Privilege (handout) (Bethesda, MD: author, 2016).

5. Adam Howard, Brianne Wheeler, and Aimee Polimeno, "Negotiating Privilege and Identity in Educational Contexts," https://1lib.us/book/ 3519280/473ee7?id=3519280&secret=473ee7 (accessed March 29, 2021).

6. Howard, Wheeler, and Polimeno, "Negotiating Privilege and Identity in Educational Contexts."

7. Ralph Waldo Emerson, Goodreads, https://www.goodreads.com/ quotes/541463-a-man-is-what-he-thinks-about-all-day-long (accessed March 26, 2021).

8. *Life of Privilege Explained in a $100 Race*, YouTube, 2019, https://www .youtube.com/watch?v=kyl4EJhq47A.

9. Jennifer M. Cook, "Social Class Bias: A Phenomenological Study," *Journal of Counselor Preparation and Supervision* 9, no. 1 (2017).

10. Cook, "Social Class Bias: A Phenomenological Study."

11. Max H. Bazerman and Don A. Moore, *Judgment In Managerial Decision Making*. 8th ed. (Hoboken, NJ: Wiley, 2013).

12. Joshua Klayman, and Young-Won Ha, "APA PsycNet," *American Psychological Association*, 1987, https://psycnet.apa.org/record/1987-20689 -001.

13. Max H. Bazerman and Don A. Moore, *Judgment In Managerial Decision Making*. 8th ed. (Hoboken, NJ: Wiley, 2013).

14. Max H. Bazerman and Don A. Moore, *Judgment In Managerial Decision Making*. 8th ed. (Hoboken, NJ: Wiley, 2013).

15. Max H. Bazerman and Don A. Moore, *Judgment In Managerial Decision Making*. 8th ed. (Hoboken, NJ: Wiley, 2013).

16. John Lingan, "Connected at the Table: The Importance of Family Meals," *Child Trends*, 2016, https://www.childtrends.org/blog/connected-at-the-table-the-importance-of-family-meals.

17. Christopher J. Gross and John Gross, conversation with my dad, November 20, 2019.

18. Saul McLeod, "Maslow's Hierarchy of Needs," *Simply Psychology*, December 29, 2020, https://www.simplypsychology.org/maslow.html#gsc.tab=0.

19. Ronald D. Davis and Eldon M. Braun, *The Gift of Dyslexia: Why Some of the Smartest People Can't Read—and How They Can Learn* (London: Souvenir Press, 2010).

20. Christopher J. Gross and Heather Kaye, conversation, July 5, 2010.

21. Christopher J. Gross and John H. Cammack, conversation, July 5, 2010.

22. Christopher S. Rugaber, "Pay Gap between College Grads and Everyone Else at a Record," *USA Today*, January 12, 2017, https://www.usatoday.com/story/money/2017/01/12/pay-gap-between-college-grads-and-everyone-else-record/96493348/.

23. Christopher J. Gross and anonymous, conversation at a professional training seminar, February 12, 2010.

24. Kunal Bhattacharya, Asim Ghosh, Daniel Monsivais, Robin I. M. Dunbar, and Kimmo Kaski, "Sex Differences in Social Focus across the Life Cycle in Humans," Royal Society Publishing, April 6, 2016, https://www.ncbi.nlm.nih.gov/pmc/articles/PMC4852646/.

25. "20 Morgan Freeman Quotes to Teach You Incredible Life Lessons," Fearless Motivation—Motivational Videos & Music, December 28, 2017, https://www.fearlessmotivation.com/2017/12/28/morgan-freeman-quotes/.

26. Earl Nightingale, *The Strangest Secret*, YouTube, 2019. https://www.youtube.com/watch?v=NbBHR_CD56M.

27. Nightingale, *Strangest Secret*.

28. *The Pursuit of Happiness Trailer*, image, 2021, https://www.youtube.com/watch?v=89Kq8SDyvfg.

29. Barbara Sher, "I Could Do Anything If I Only Knew What It Was," 2021, https://www.penguinrandomhouse.com/books/165781/i-could-do-anything-if-i-only-knew-what-it-was-by-barbara-sher-with-barbara-smith/.

30. Zig Ziglar, *Goals: Setting And Achieving Them On Schedule*, directed/performed by Zig Ziglar (July 1, 1988; Manhattan: Simon & Schuster Audio/Nightingale-Conant, 2002), Audio CD.

CHAPTER 3

1. 50 Cent and Robert Greene, *The 50th Law*, 2009.

2. "Social Norms—Biases & Heuristics," Decision Lab, February 26, 2021, https://thedecisionlab.com/biases/social-norms/?utm_term=social+norms&utm_campaign=Biases&utm_medium=ppc&utm_source=adwords&hsa_kw=social+norms&hsa_ver=3&hsa_src=g&hsa_mt=b&hsa_cam=1044459117&hsa_tgt=kwd-328890627993&hsa_ad=422991074777&hsa_net=adwords&hsa_grp=79630447884&hsa_acc=8441935193&gclid=CjwKCAjwtdeFBhBAEiwAKOIy51oB3Hc6NxjC9gN-6RvQYfd_MePyWtpWnRMcvZKgQoNX8fYuRxSmctBoC9NwQAvD_BwE.

3. Angeline Vuong, "The Role of People of Color in the Future Workforce," Center for American Progress, December 11, 2013, https://www.americanprogress.org/issues/immigration/news/2013/10/25/77924/the-role-of-people-of-color-in-the-future-workforce/.

CHAPTER 4

1. Criss Jami, *Killosophy*, Goodreads, https://www.goodreads.com/work/quotes/43973648-killosophy (accessed April 22, 2021).

2. Jan De Houwer, "Implicit Bias Is Behavior: A Functional-Cognitive Perspective on Implicit Bias—Jan De Houwer, 2019," Sage Journals, https://journals.sagepub.com/doi/10.1177/1745691619855638#:~:text=More%20specifically%2C%20implicit%20bias%20can,group%20to%20which%20others%20belong. Accessed July 30, 2021.

3. Houwer, "Implicit Bias Is Behavior."

4. Max H. Bazerman and Don A. Moore, *Judgment in Managerial Decision Making*, 8th ed. (Hoboken, NJ: Wiley, 2013).

5. Daniel Kahneman, *Thinking, Fast and Slow*, 1st ed. (New York: Farrar, Straus & Giroux, 2011).

6. Jess M. Stein, Stuart Berg Flexner, Enid Pearsons, and Carol G. Braham. *Random House Roget's College Thesaurus* (New York: Random House, 2001).

7. Bazerman and Moore, *Judgment in Managerial Decision Making*, 8th ed. (Hoboken, NJ: Wiley, 2013).

8. Katye Vytal, "Learning to Fear," Association for Psychological Science, January 1, 2007, https://www.psychologicalscience.org/observer/learning-to-fear.

9. Christopher J. Gross and anonymous, conversation with a colleague about the function of bias, n.d.

10. Jennifer Pharr, Carol Irwin, Todd Layne, and Richard Irwin, "Predictors of Swimming Ability among Children and Adolescents in the United States," *Sports* 6, no. 1 (2018): 17, https://doi.org/10.3390/sports6010017.

11. Bruce Wigo, February 5, 2019, "The Importance of 'A Film Called Blacks Can't Swim,'" *Swimming World News*, February 6, 2019, https://www.swimmingworldmagazine.com/news/the-importance-of-a-film-called-Blacks-cant-swim/.

CHAPTER 5

1. Christopher J. Gross and Howard Ross, conversation about Ross's company values, inner work, n.d.

2. "From the Ground Up," Iyanla Vanzant (blog), https://iyanla.com/groundup/ (accessed May 10, 2021).

3. C. G. Jung, Goodreads, https://www.goodreads.com/quotes/39433-your-visions-will-become-clear-only-when-you-can-look (accessed May 10, 2021).

4. "From the Ground Up," Iyanla Vanzant.

5. "More Black Men Embracing Yoga to Ease Emotional Stress," NBC News, https://www.nbcnews.com/news/nbcblk/more-black-men-embracing-yoga-ease-emotional-stress-n1100836 (accessed May 12, 2021).

6. Christopher J. Gross and Eddie, speaking about cars, n.d.

7. Kenji Yoshino, *Covering: The Hidden Assault On Our Civil Rights* (New York: Random House, 2007).

8. Stephen R. Covey, *The 7 Habits of Highly Effective People* (New York: Simon & Schuster, 2017).

9. Christopher J. Gross and Howard Ross, conversation about Ross's company values, inner work, n.d.

10. Henri Tajfel, and Jerome S. Bruner, *Human Groups and Social Categories* (Cambridge: Cambridge University Press, 1981).

11. "Empathy Connects, Sympathy Disconnects," Interaction Institute for Social Change, December 13, 2013, https://interactioninstitute.org/empathy-connects-sympathy-disconnects/.

12. "Emotional Intelligence Is No Soft Skill," Professional Development/Harvard DCE, July 6, 2015, https://professional.dce.harvard.edu/blog/emotional-intelligence-is-no-soft-skill/.

13. "From the Ground Up," Iyanla Vanzant.

CHAPTER 6

1. Theresa Agovino, "Companies Try a New Approach to Diversity, Equity and Inclusion: Honest Conversations," SHRM, August 28, 2020, https://www.shrm.org/hr-today/news/hr-magazine/fall2020/pages/a-new-approach-to-diversity-and-inclusion.aspx.

2. Christopher J. Gross and Johnnetta B. Cole, conversation about diversity, March 3, 2018.

3. Christopher J. Gross and Howard Ross, "Belonging is when you get to choose the music," n.d.

4. Sylvia A. Hewlett, Melinda Marshall, and Laura Sherbin, "How Diversity Can Drive Innovation," *Harvard Business Review*, December 2013, https://hbr.org/2013/12/how-diversity-can-drive-innovation.

5. Hewlett, Marshall, and Sherbin, "How Diversity Can Drive Innovation."

6. Hewlett, Marshall, and Sherbin, "How Diversity Can Drive Innovation."

7. Hewlett, Marshall, and Sherbin, "How Diversity Can Drive Innovation."

8. Lou Solomon, "Becoming Powerful Makes You Less Empathetic," *Harvard Business Review*, April 21, 2015, https://hbr.org/2015/04/becoming-powerful-makes-you-less-empathetic.

9. Solomon, "Becoming Powerful Makes You Less Empathetic."

10. Elizabeth A. Segal, "Power Blocks Empathy," *Psychology Today*, https://www.psychologytoday.com/us/blog/social-empathy/201909/power-blocks-empathy (accessed July 8, 2021).

11. Segal, "Power Blocks Empathy."

12. Segal, "Power Blocks Empathy."

13. Maggie Koerth, "A Half-Day of Diversity Training Won't Change Much for Starbucks," FiveThirtyEight, May 29, 2018, https://fivethirtyeight.com/features/a-half-day-of-diversity-training-wont-change-much-for-starbucks/.

14. Koerth, "A Half-Day of Diversity Training Won't Change Much for Starbucks."

15. Christopher J. Gross and VP of construction management company, "Well, we've devoted more marketing to the colleges that we recruit from," n.d.

16. Christopher J. Gross and VP of construction management company, "What do you mean where else? I just told you these are the three schools that we recruit from," n.d.

17. Christopher J. Gross and VP of construction management company, "Not really, because I really don't know anyone there," n.d.

18. Arshiya Malik, "These 19 Companies Are Connecting Employers to Diverse Pools of Talent," Medium, January 7, 2021, https://medium.com/aleria/these-19-companies-are-connecting-employers-to-diverse-pools-of-talent-3e902c7d9208.

19. Larry Prusack, "What Can't Be Measured," *Harvard Business Review*, July 23, 2014, https://hbr.org/2010/10/what-cant-be-measured.

20. Christopher J. Gross and Dr. Lynn Scott, "If you want people to be more inclusive, tie it to their compensation plan and promotion evaluation," n.d.

21. Paolo Gaudiano, "Inclusion Is Invisible: How To Measure It," *Forbes*, April 25, 2019, https://www.forbes.com/sites/paologaudiano/2019/04/23/inclusion-is-invisible-how-to-measure-it/?sh=5ba1ec15a3d2.

22. Serena Olsaretti, "Introduction: The Idea of Distributive Justice," Oxford Handbooks Online, May 31, 2018, https://www.oxfordhandbooks.com/view/10.1093/oxfordhb/9780199645121.001.0001/oxfordhb-9780199645121-e-38#oxfordhb-9780199645121-e-38-bibItem-17.

23. Cary Funk and Kim Parker, "Diversity in the STEM Workforce Varies Widely across Jobs," Pew Research Center's Social & Demographic Trends Project, December 31, 2019, https://www.pewresearch.org/social-trends/2018/01/09/diversity-in-the-stem-workforce-varies-widely-across-jobs/.

24. "Workplace Mentoring Supplement to the Elements of Effective Practice for Mentoring™," *Mentor*, August 27, 2020, https://www.mentoring.org/resource/workplace-mentoring/.

CHAPTER 7

1. Saul McLeod, "Maslow's Hierarchy of Needs," *Simply Psychology*, December 29, 2020, http://www.simplypsychology.org/maslow.html.

2. Mitchell Beck and James Malley, "A Pedagogy of Belonging," International Child and Youth Care Network, 1998, https://cyc-net.org/cyc-online/cycol-0303-belonging.html.

3. John Steinbeck, *East of Eden* (New York: Penguin, 1952).

4. Beck and Malley, "A Pedagogy of Belonging."

5. Beck and Malley, "A Pedagogy of Belonging."

6. Harriet Over, "The Origins of Belonging: Social Motivation in Infants and Young Children," Royal Society Publishing, July 6, 2015, https://royalsocietypublishing.org/doi/pdf/10.1098/rstb.2015.0072.

7. Christopher J. Gross and Nathaniel, conversation at the sporting goods store, n.d.

8. Cartwright, Doug. 2021. "25 Popular Brené Brown Quotes on Empathy, Shame, and Trust." www.thedailyshifts.com. April 2, 2021.

9. Kenji Yoshino, *Covering: The Hidden Assault on Our Civil Rights* (New York: Random House, 2007),

10. Stephen R. Covey, *The 7 Habits of Highly Effective People* (New York: Simon & Schuster, 2017).

11. Covey, *7 Habits of Highly Effective People.*

12. Henri Tajfel, *Human Groups and Social Categories* (Cambridge: Cambridge University Press, 1981).

13. R. F. Baumeister and M. R. Leary, "The Need to Belong: Desire for Interpersonal Attachments as a Fundamental Human Emotion," *Psychological Bulletin*, 112 (1995): 461–84; R. M. Lee and S. B. Robbins, "The

Relationship between Social Connectedness and Anxiety, Self-Esteem, and Social Identity," *Journal of Counseling Psychology,* 45 (1998): 338–45.

CHAPTER 8

1. "Diversity and Inclusion Timeline," Center for Talent Innovation, https://www.talentinnovation.org/assets/DiversityAndInclusionTime line-CTI.pdf (accessed July 12, 2021).

2. Mike Cummings, "Yale Study Shows Class Bias in Hiring Based on Few Seconds of Speech," *YaleNews,* October 21, 2019, https://news.yale .edu/2019/10/21/yale-study-shows-class-bias-hiring-based-few-seconds -speech.

3. "What Is the Role of a Mentor?" Do-It, https://www.washington .edu/doit/what-role-mentor (accessed July 12, 2021).

4. Glenn Parker and Michael Parker, https://thepositiveinfluenceleader .com/ (accessed July 19, 2021).

5. *One of the Greatest Speeches Ever,* YouTube, https://www.youtube .com/watch?v=NQ4en7o8B-g (accessed July 19, 2021).

6. Christopher J. Gross and Ekaterina Dyspikinam, interview, n.d.

7. Christopher J. Gross and Howard Ross, rationale behind workplace appearance, n.d.

8. Christopher J. Gross and Howard Ross, "Sometimes people did not come to me for the kind of support that I could provide them because they were afraid that I would be looking down on them," n.d.

9. Christopher J. Gross and Dr. Lynn Scott, "What does she like to do?," n.d.

10. Christopher J. Gross and Howard Ross, "From day one, you were like a sponge, and that is inspiring," n.d.

11. Miriam Wallack, "5 Mentorship Companies Showcasing the Best Mentorship Programs," Gloat, June 16, 2021, https://www.gloat.com/ blog/5-companies-showcasing-successful-mentorship-programs/.

12. Christopher J. Gross and John, communication about time and resources and their possible constraints on opportunity from John's perspective, June 20, 2020.

Bibliography

Agovino, Theresa. "Companies Try a New Approach to Diversity, Equity and Inclusion: Honest Conversations." SHRM, August 28, 2020. https://www.shrm.org/hr-today/news/hr-magazine/fall2020/pages/a-new-approach-to-diversity-and-inclusion.aspx.

Anonymous. "If you can't see it, you can't be it" (accessed August 4, 2017).

Bachhuber, Thomas. "NetWorking: Rich Is More Than Money." Center for Life Transitions, March 19, 2019. https://www.centerforlifetransitions.net/2013/networking-rich-is-more-than-money/#:~:text=Robert%20Kiyosaki%20says%2C%20%E2%80%9CThe%20richest,because%20they%20have%20a%20job.

Baumeister, R. F., and M. R. Leary. "The Need to Belong: Desire for Interpersonal Attachments as a Fundamental Human Emotion." *Psychological Bulletin*, 112 (1995): 461–84.

Bazerman, Max H., and Don A. Moore. *Judgment in Managerial Decision Making*, 8th ed. Hoboken, NJ: Wiley, 2013.

———. *Managerial Decision Making in Censored Environments: Biased Judgment of Demand, Risk, And Employee Capability*, 8th ed. Hoboken, NJ: Wiley, 2012.

Beck, Mitchell, and James Malley. "A Pedagogy of Belonging." International Child and Youth Care Network, 1998. https://cyc-net.org/cyc-online/cycol-0303-belonging.html.

Bhattacharya, Kunal, Asim Ghosh, Daniel Monsivais, Robin I. M. Dunbar, and Kimmo Kaski. "Sex Differences in Social Focus across the Life Cycle

in Humans." Royal Society Publishing, April 6, 2016. https://www.ncbi
.nlm.nih.gov/pmc/articles/PMC4852646/.

Cartwright, Doug. "25 Popular Brené Brown Quotes On Empathy, Shame,
And Trust." www.thedailyshifts.com, April 2, 2021. https://www.
thedailyshifts.com/blog/25-popular-brene-brown-quotes-on-empathy
-shame-and-trust.

Cent, 50, and Robert Greene. *The 50th Law*, 2009.

Chen, C. "On the Shoulders of Giants," in *Mapping Scientific Frontiers: The
Quest for Knowledge Visualization*. Springer, London, 2003, https://doi
.org/10.1007/978-1-4471-0051-5_5.

Chung, Hae-Kyung, Hye Jeong Yang, Dayeon Shin, and Kyung Rhan
Chung. "Aesthetics of Korean Foods: The Symbol of Korean Culture."
Journal of Ethnic Foods 3, no. 3 (2016): 178–88. https://doi.org/10.1016/j
.jef.2016.09.001.

Clark, Kim, and Ian Johnson. "TOUGH ENOUGH: Jean Fugett's Toughest
Job Yet: Replacing Brother Reginald Lewis at TLC Beatrice." baltimore-
sun.com, January 31, 1993. http://www.baltimoresun.com/news/bs
-xpm-1993-01-31-1993031121-story.html (accessed October 24, 2018).

Cook, Jennifer M. "Social Class Bias: A Phenomenological Study." *Journal of
Counselor Preparation and Supervision* 9, no. 1 (2017).

Covey, Stephen R. *The 7 Habits of Highly Effective People*. New York: Simon
& Schuster, 2017.

Cross, Rob, and Robert J. Thomas. "Managing Yourself: A Smarter Way
to Network." *Harvard Business Review*, September 7, 2017. https://hbr
.org/2011/07/managing-yourself-a-smarter-way-to-network.

Cummings, Mike. "Yale Study Shows Class Bias in Hiring Based on
Few Seconds of Speech." *YaleNews*, October 21, 2019. https://news
.yale.edu/2019/10/21/yale-study-shows-class-bias-hiring-based-few
-seconds-speech.

"The Dagobah Cave: A Figurative Exploration." StarWars.com, October 22, 2014. https://www.starwars.com/news/studying-skywalkers
-figuratively-exploring-the-dagobah-cave.

Davis, Ronald D., and Eldon M. Braun. *The Gift of Dyslexia: Why Some of the
Smartest People Can't Read—and How They Can Learn*. London: Souvenir
Press, 2010.

"Diversity and Inclusion Timeline." Center for Talent Innovation, https://
www.talentinnovation.org/assets/DiversityAndInclusionTimeline-CTI.
pdf (accessed July 12, 2021).

Em, David, "50+ Unforgettable John Wooden Quotes." Next Level Gents,
December 11, 2021. https://nextlevelgents.com/john-wooden-quotes/.

Emerson, Ralph Waldo. Goodreads. https://www.goodreads.com/quotes/
541463-a-man-is-what-he-thinks-about-all-day-long (accessed March 26,
2021).

"Emotional Intelligence Is No Soft Skill." Professional Development/ Harvard DCE, July 6, 2015. https://professional.dce.harvard.edu/blog/ emotional-intelligence-is-no-soft-skill/.

"Empathy Connects, Sympathy Disconnects." Interaction Institute for Social Change, December 13, 2013. https://interactioninstitute.org/ empathy-connects-sympathy-disconnects/.

Follin, Mary. "Celebrating a Legacy: Father and Son Share Insights at Special Event." *GW Alumni News*, July 12, 2016. www.gwalumni.org/2016/06/ celebrating-a-legacy-father-and-son-to-share-insights-at-special-event/.

"From the Ground Up." Iyanla Vanzant (blog). https://iyanla.com/ groundup/ (accessed May 10, 2021).

Funk, Cary, and Kim Parker. "Diversity in the STEM Workforce Varies Widely across Jobs." Pew Research Center's Social & Demographic Trends Project, December 31, 2019. https://www.pewresearch.org/ social-trends/2018/01/09/diversity-in-the-stem-workforce-varies -widely-across-jobs/.

Gaudiano, Paolo. "Inclusion Is Invisible: How to Measure It." *Forbes*, April 25, 2019. https://www.forbes.com/sites/paologaudiano/2019/04/23/ inclusion-is-invisible-how-to-measure-it/?sh=5ba1ec15a3d2.

Hewlett, Sylvia A., Melinda Marshall, and Laura Sherbin. "How Diversity Can Drive Innovation." *Harvard Business Review*, December 2013. https:// hbr.org/2013/12/how-diversity-can-drive-innovation.

Houwer, Jan De. "Implicit Bias Is Behavior: A Functional-Cognitive Perspective on Implicit Bias—Jan De Houwer, 2019." Sage Journals. https://journals.sagepub.com/doi/10.1177/1745691619855834#:~:text =More%20specifically%2C%20implicit%20bias%20can,group%20to%20 which%20others%20belong (accessed July 30, 2021).

Howard, Adam, Brianne Wheeler, and Aimee Polimeno. "Negotiating Privilege and Identity in Educational Contexts." https://1lib.us/book/ 3519280/473ee7?id=3519280&secret=473ee7 (accessed March 29, 2021).

Jami, Criss. *Killosophy*. Goodreads. https://www.goodreads.com/work/ quotes/43973648-killosophy (accessed April 22, 2021).

Jung, C. G. Goodreads. https://www.goodreads.com/quotes/39433-your -visions-will-become-clear-only-when-you-can-look (accessed May 10, 2021).

Kahneman, Daniel. *Thinking, Fast and Slow*, 1st ed. New York: Farrar, Straus & Giroux, 2011.

Kiyosaki, Robert T. "Rich Dad Poor Dad: With Updates for Today's World—and 9 New Study Session Sections." 2017. https://www.amazon .com/Rich-Dad-Poor-Teach-Middle/dp/1612680194.

Klayman, Joshua, and Young-Won Ha. "APA PsycNet." *American Psychological Association*, 1987. https://psycnet.apa.org/record/1987-20689-001.

Koerth, Maggie. "A Half-Day of Diversity Training Won't Change Much for Starbucks." FiveThirtyEight, May 29, 2018. https://fivethirtyeight

.com / features / a-half-day-of-diversity-training-wont-change-much-for
-starbucks /.

Kraus, Michael W., Jun Won Park, and Jacinth J. Tan. "Signs of Social Class: The Experience of Economic Inequality in Everyday Life." *Perspectives on Psychological Science* 12, no. 3 (2017): 422–35. https:// doi .org/10.1177/1745691616673192.

Lee, R. M., and S. B. Robbins. "The Relationship between Social Connectedness and Anxiety, Self-Esteem, and Social Identity." *Journal of Counseling Psychology*, 45 (1998): 338–45.

Lewis, Reginald F., and Blair Walker. "The Higher Education of the Late Reginald F. Lewis." *Journal of Blacks in Higher Education*, no. 8 (1995): 84–87. doi:10.2307/2963061 (accessed March 29, 2021).

Life of Privilege Explained in a $100 Race. YouTube, 2019. https:// www.youtube.com / watch?v=kyl4EJhq47A.

Lingan, John. "Connected at the Table: The Importance of Family Meals." *Child Trends*, 2016. https:// www.childtrends.org/ blog/ connected-at-the -table-the-importance-of-family-meals.

Malik, Arshiya. "These 19 Companies Are Connecting Employers to Diverse Pools of Talent." Medium, January 7, 2021. https:// medium.com / aleria/ these-19-companies-are-connecting-employers-to-diverse-pools-of-talent -3e902c7d9208.

McCauley, Mary Carole. "Reginald Lewis' Daughter Opens Up about Growing Up with Her Famous Father." baltimoresun.com, June 19, 2018. https:// www.baltimoresun.com / entertainment / arts / bs-ae-lewis -memoir-20120210-story.html.

McLeod, Saul. "Maslow's Hierarchy of Needs." *Simply Psychology*, December 29, 2020. http:// www.simplypsychology.org / maslow.html.

"More Black Men Embracing Yoga to Ease Emotional Stress." NBC News. https:// www.nbcnews.com / news / nbcblk / more-black-men-embracing -yoga-ease-emotional-stress-n1100836 (accessed May 12, 2021).

Muchinsky, Paul M. "The Power and Influence Approach," in *Psychology Applied to Work: An Introduction to Industrial and Organizational Psychology*, 10th ed. (Summerfield, NC: Hypergraphic Press, 2012), 401–2.

National Association of School Psychologists. *Understanding Race and Privilege* (handout). Bethesda, MD: author, 2016.

"Networking Sayings and Networking Quotes." https:// www.wisesayings .com / networking-quotes/ (accessed March 30, 2021).

Nightingale, Earl. *The Strangest Secret*. YouTube, 2019. https:// www.you tube.com / watch?v=NbBHR_CD56M.

O'Donnell, Katy. "Leslie Sword's Vision." baltimoresun.com, October 27, 2018. https:// www.baltimoresun.com / news / bs-xpm-2007-12-02 -0711220087-story.html.

Olsaretti, Serena. "Introduction: The Idea of Distributive Justice." Oxford Handbooks Online, May 31, 2018. https:// www.oxfordhandbooks

.com / view / 10.1093 / oxfordhb / 9780199645121.001.0001 / oxfordhb
-9780199645121-e-38# oxfordhb-9780199645121-e-38-bibItem-17.

One of the Greatest Speeches Ever. YouTube. https: / / www.youtube.com /
watch?v=NQ4en7o8B-g (accessed July 19, 2021).

Over, Harriet. "The Origins of Belonging: Social Motivation in Infants and
Young Children." Royal Society Publishing, July 6, 2015. https: / / royalso-
cietypublishing.org / doi / pdf / 10.1098 / rstb.2015.0072.

Parker, Glenn, and Michael Parker. https: / / thepositiveinfluenceleader
.com / (accessed July 19, 2021).

Parkin, Alan. "Social Class: Historical Origins and Psychological Influences." *Canadian Psychiatric Association Journal* 7, no. 4 (August 1962):
178–85. https: / / doi.org / 10.1177 / 070674376200700407.

Pharr, Jennifer, Carol Irwin, Todd Layne, and Richard Irwin. "Predictors
of Swimming Ability among Children and Adolescents in the United
States." *Sports* 6, no. 1 (2018): 17. https: / / doi.org / 10.3390 / sports6010017.

Prusack, Larry. "What Can't Be Measured." *Harvard Business Review*,
July 23, 2014. https: / / hbr.org / 2010 / 10 / what-cant-be-measured.

The Pursuit of Happiness Trailer. image, 2021. https: / / www.youtube.com /
watch?v=89Kq8SDyvfg.

Ripley, Sam, "60 Mentor Quotes Celebrating Guidance & Inspiration."
Everyday Power. everydaypower.com, March 10, 2021. https: / / everyday
power.com / mentor-quotes /.

Romano, Nick. "Jimmy Kimmel Comes to Terms with His Own White Privilege." EW.com, June 3, 2020. https: / / ew.com / tv / jimmy-kimmel-white
-privilege / (accessed March 29, 2021).

Rugaber, Christopher S. "Pay Gap between College Grads and Everyone
Else at a Record." *USA Today*, January 12, 2017. https: / / www.usatoday
.com / story / money / 2017 / 01 / 12 / pay-gap-between-college-grads-and
-everyone-else-record / 96493348 /.

Segal, Elizabeth A. "Power Blocks Empathy." *Psychology Today*. https: / /
www.psychologytoday.com / us / blog / social-empathy / 201909 / power
-blocks-empathy (accessed July 8, 2021).

Sher, Barbara. "I Could Do Anything If I Only Knew What It Was,"
2021. https: / / www.penguinrandomhouse.com / books / 165781 / i-could
-do-anything-if-i-only- knew-what-it-was-by-barbara-sher-with-barbara
-smith /.

"Social Norms—Biases & Heuristics." Decision Lab, February 26,
2021. https: / / thedecisionlab.com / biases / social-norms / ?utm_
term=social+norms&utm_campaign=Biases&utm_medium=ppc&utm_
source=adwords&hsa_kw=social+norms&hsa_ver=3&hsa_src=
g&hsa_mt=b&hsa_cam=1044459117&hsa_tgt=kwd-328890627993&hsa_
ad=422991074777&hsa_net=adwords&hsa_grp=79630447884&hsa_acc=
8441935193&gclid=CjwKCAjwtdeFBhBAEiwAKOIy51oB3Hc6NxjC9gN

6RvQYfd_MePyWtpWnRMcvZKgQoNX8fYuRxSmctBoC9NwQAvD_
BwE.

Solomon, Lou. "Becoming Powerful Makes You Less Empathetic." *Harvard
Business Review*, April 21, 2015. https://hbr.org/2015/04/becoming
-powerful-makes-you-less-empathetic.

Stein, Jess M., Stuart Berg Flexner, Enid Pearsons, and Carol G. Braham.
Random House Roget's College Thesaurus. New York: Random House, 2001.

Steinbeck, John. *East of Eden*. New York: Penguin, 1952.

Tajfel, Henri. *Human Groups and Social Categories*. Cambridge: Cambridge
University Press, 1981.

"Thurgood Marshall—A Century of Upstanders." https://sites.google
.com/a/ntfh.cmsdnet.net/a-century-of-upstanders2/your-person
-s-name/civil-rights-era/thurgood-marshall (accessed March 30, 2021).

"20 Morgan Freeman Quotes to Teach You Incredible Life Lessons." Fearless
Motivation—Motivational Videos & Music, December 28, 2017. https://
www.fearlessmotivation.com/2017/12/28/morgan-freeman-quotes/.

Vuong, Angeline. "The Role of People of Color in the Future Workforce."
Center for American Progress, December 11, 2013. https://www.ameri
canprogress.org/issues/immigration/news/2013/10/25/77924/the
-role-of-people-of-color-in-the-future-workforce/.

Vytal, Katye. "Learning to Fear." *Association for Psychological Science*, January 1, 2007. https://www.psychologicalscience.org/observer/learning
-to-fear.

Walker, Alice. "'The Most Common Way People Give Up Their Power Is by
Thinking They Don't Have Any." Good News Network, March 10, 2021.
https://www.goodnewsnetwork.org/alice-walker-quote-about-power/.

Wallack, Miriam. "5 Mentorship Companies Showcasing the Best Mentorship Programs." Gloat, June 16, 2021. https://www.gloat.com/blog/5
-companies-showcasing-successful-mentorship-programs/.

"What Is the Role of a Mentor?" Do-It. https://www.washington.edu/
doit/what-role-mentor (accessed July 12, 2021).

Wheeler, Aimee Polimeno. https://1lib.us/book/3519280/473ee7?id=3519
280&secret=473ee7 (accessed March 29, 2021).

Wigo, Bruce. "The Importance of 'A Film Called Blacks Can't Swim.'" *Swimming World News*, February 6, 2019. https://www.swimmingworldmaga
zine.com/news/the-importance-of-a-film-called-blacks-cant-swim/.

Wilkie, Dana. "Employers Say Students Aren't Learning Soft Skills in College." SHRM, February 28, 2020. www.shrm.org/resourcesandtools/
hr-topics/employee-relations/pages/employers-say-students-arent
-learning-soft-skills-in-college.aspx.

Williams, Joan C. *White Working Class: Overcoming Class Cluelessness in
America* (Boston, MA: Harvard Business Review Press, 2017).

Williams, Joan C., Marina Multhaup, and Sky Mihaylo. "Why Companies
Should Add Class to Their Diversity Discussions." *Harvard Business*

Review, September 5, 2018. https://hbr.org/2018/09/why-companies
-should-add-class-to-their-diversity-discussions.

"Workplace Mentoring Supplement to the Elements of Effective Practice for
Mentoring™." *Mentor,* August 27, 2020. https://www.mentoring.org/
resource/workplace-mentoring/.

Yan, Holly. "What We Know So Far in the College Admissions Cheating
Scandal." *CNN,* March 19, 2019. www.cnn.com/2019/03/13/us/what
-we-know-college-admissions-cheating-scandal/index.html.

Yoshino, Kenji. *Covering: The Hidden Assault on Our Civil Rights.* New York:
Random House, 2007.

Ziglar, Zig. *Goals: Setting and Achieving Them on Schedule.* directed/
performed by Zig Ziglar (July 1, 1988; New York: Simon & Schuster
Audio/Nightingale-Conant, 2002), Audio CD.

Index

About the Author

Christopher "CJ" Gross is a TEDx speaker, international organizational development consultant, and founder of Ascension Worldwide, a full-service minority-owned consulting firm committed to helping clients achieve workplace inclusion, and employee and client diversity. He has eighteen years of experience working with Fortune 500 companies, local and national nonprofits, and government agencies. He also serves as a business management, adjunct faculty for the Community College of Baltimore County and a diversity, equity, and inclusion master faculty for the University of Maryland, Baltimore County, Center for Innovation. CJ is a former mechanical designer with General Electric, avid traveler, and adventure junkie living in Shrewsbury, Pennsylvania, with his wife, Kerryann. Together they have three children who are attending college.